W9-AHZ-080

UNSHAKABLE

THE REMARKABLE TRUE STORY OF
RICK SILANSKAS

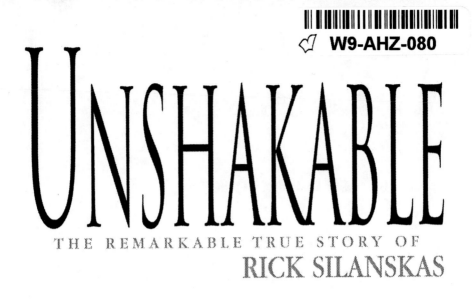

Advantage
BOOKS

PAULA FELPS

Unshakable by Paula Felps
© 2005 by The Project Anna Foundation
All Rights Reserved.
ISBN: 1-59755-034-5

Published by: ADVANTAGE BOOKS™
www.advbooks.com

This book and parts thereof may not be reproduced in any form, stored in a retrieval system or transmitted in any form by any means (electronic, mechanical, photocopy, recording or otherwise) without prior written permission of the author, except as provided by United States of America copyright law.

Library of Congress Control Number: 2005931511

First Printing: November 2005

11 12 01 02 03 04   9 8 7 6 5 4 3 2 1

Printed in the United States of America

DEDICATION

This book is dedicated to all the orphaned children of Russia. Theirs are the eyes of a million souls who look to us, the world, to care, just…care.

If I could, I would hold each child in my arms and say to them: *"My heart is your father, my faith is your strength, my love is your hope, my body is your servant, my God is your family."*

Rick Silanskas

Paula Felps

FOREWORD

When I was asked to write the foreword for this book I could not say "yes" fast enough! First of all, I already knew the blessed events that surround this compelling story, and secondly, I wished everyone could be exposed to this adventure of the heart so that each might be inspired to listen closely for God's calling in their own lives…and respond!

As you read this extraordinary story of actual events you cannot help but feel your heart expand with deep-felt emotion. That lump in your throat will let you know you are experiencing something rare, something just beyond our understanding…something God has touched with His love. The circumstances will astound you and open your spirit to new possibilities in life! If God were to challenge you to exercise more strength, more courage, more faith in daily life, what would you do? This book is about how one man responded to just such a challenge – even though it meant profound changes to his life and the lives of his entire family!

Rick Silanskas and his wife Stephanie had already raised four children. Two were in college and two were teenagers. Soon the couple would enjoy the freedoms that come with bringing young ones to their age of independence. But then something both frightening and wondrous happened to Rick that would lead to the greatest challenge of his life. He would overcome seemingly insurmountable cultural and legal obstacles in one of the world's most powerful nations in his mission to save the life of one small, innocent girl.

The dynamic forces that would bring this child to the shores of America and into the arms of Rick's loving family can only be described as "miraculous!" I know as you read this book you will find yourself wondering, "Can this be true? Could this have really happened?" Well, let me tell you about Rick Silanskas. He's a stand-up guy with a steel will, an abiding faith, a heart of gold and an inspiring story to tell.

It was my privilege to hear Rick relate the incredible circumstances of his experience when he was invited to speak at our Sunday morning Bible Study at First Baptist Church in Orlando, Florida. The intense love he expressed for this child he had never even met, and his unwavering commitment to finding her somewhere in the world and bringing her home, captivated the hearts of his audience and literally brought tears to our eyes.

Now, I'll admit I'm a good listener but I'm not a "pushover" as an audience. In sharing the stage with the Rev. Billy Graham as a speaker at two of his national crusades, being a guest on Dr. Robert Schuller's televised "Hour of Power," performing well over one hundred speaking engagements a year and hosting a sports radio show, you can imagine I've heard and told a lot of stories! But the powerful message of Rick's testimony, his devotion to the concept of family, the tears that he shared with us that day over his search for his missing "daughter"- that's how he thought of her - compelled me to approach Rick after his talk and urge him to tell his story of how God guided him through his darkest hours and into the light of a child's love in a way that would reach more people. The book you hold in your hands is the result.

I felt an immediate kinship with Rick and his family because I have been blessed with fourteen adopted children from four countries in addition to my own five, and we love each of them with all our hearts. Even when their search was over, we know the gut-wrenching pain Rick and Stephanie must have felt when the process wore on. They knew that each passing day meant another day of suffering and loneliness for this baby girl who was wasting away with little human contact, abandoned by her mother to an under-funded, understaffed orphanage in the remotest part of Russia.

By story's end you will be inspired and heartened by the results of one man's actions that began on behalf of a single child, and wound up touching the hearts of countless children that otherwise would be living without love and without hope.

The hand of God is truly revealed in the details of this journey…a journey of self-discovery, of unwavering strength and of a power that transcends the international borders of former cold-war enemies, and unites the hearts of two nations in the common cause of His love.

Good reading and God's best to you,

Pat Williams
Senior Vice President
Orlando Magic

Paula Felps

Preface

When I left my job as managing editor of a national music magazine in 1998, the reason behind my resignation was simple – I felt that there was something else I had to do. I have written for as long as I can remember, penning stories almost from the moment I learned how to string words together. By the third grade, I was writing "books" and creating Crayola-and-construction paper covers for them. It wasn't as if I made a conscious decision to become a writer; it was just what I was born to do.

The writing path led me to journalism school, then to the expected ladder of newspapers, beginning with a small weekly and moving on to a daily paper. As a reporter, I had the chance to hone a wide array of skills, covering everything from the police blotter to city council meetings to human-interest features. At times I could see glimmers of what had driven me to pursue reporting. It's the same thing that drives most writers to take notoriously low-paying newspaper jobs and work insanely long hours: We feel as if we can somehow make a difference. There were moments when I felt that was true – there were stories on throw-away kids; award-winning reports on the crumbling healthcare system; feature stories on individuals who truly inspired me. But then, inevitably, the daily grind of filling a newspaper would rear its ugly head, reminding me that my passion had become a job.

Eventually I began covering music, something I truly loved, and ended up immersing myself in entertainment writing. That inevitably led to editors' positions that ultimately made me realize how far I was from where – and why – I had begun this journey. So, with just a handful of possibilities and a huge leap of faith, I quit my job and returned to writing. "That's such a cool job!" people would remark. "Why did you leave it?"

I would just tell them that I believed I had more to say in life than who was on drums, bass and guitar. As it turns out, that assumption was correct.

My first encounter with Rick Silanskas was a two-hour phone call for a brief piece in *Private Clubs* magazine. In the years since becoming a full-time freelance writer, I had met fascinating people and had written about an exhilarating range of topics, but none of them quite compared to the story that Rick had to tell. The editor at *Private Clubs* sent me a DVD called "Nadia's Story," which is a documentary that chronicles his amazing chain of events. I was moved by what I saw, and as Rick and I spoke, the emotion of the story still bubbled through his voice.

I had everything I needed for my short assignment in the first 20 minutes, but we continued talking. There was so much more to this story than could be expressed in the space the magazine had allotted! I managed to pare it down to the word count I'd been assigned, but Rick and I stayed in touch. We talked again when the article appeared in the magazine. I told Rick that I felt there was so much more that could be done with this story; I truly felt like it needed to be told in full.

Rick called me in June 2004, about a month after the story appeared in *Private Clubs*. Pat Williams, a well-known author in his own right, had heard Rick's story and now was encouraging him to write the book. Would I, Rick wanted to know, be interested in writing it?

There wasn't a moment's hesitation. I knew I had plenty left to learn from this story. Fortunately, I already had a trip to Florida planned for the following month. Our first meeting included Nadia, Rick's wife Stephanie and Ludmilla, the Russian translator who has become a part of their family in so many ways. In a summer and fall scarred by hurricanes, we worked around the storms and the chaos they created to put Rick's miraculous journey on paper. The hurricanes created frequent and numerous delays to our original plan, but eventually we were able to create a routine and begin talking regularly about the path that had brought Rick to this point in his life.

It's an amazing process to re-live the most important events of someone else's life and it is an emotional experience for both parties. In working with Rick to explore and share his story, it was impossible not to look at my own life. As a writer studying someone else's life, I found myself studying my own. How many times have I felt called to do something, but ignored it out of fear? For that matter, how often does each of us drown out the still, small voice of God, hearing instead the cacophony of the world in which we live?

"Unshakable" is an incredible story of faith and about learning to listen. It is more than the story of a miraculous dream and the man who followed it with steadfast faith. It is the story of our ability to change our lives and the lives of those around us by doing two very simple but difficult things: listening and following. In writing this book, I learned something about doing both. And I finally found the story that I'd been waiting all these years to write.

Paula Felps

Paula Felps

Chapter One

Despite the balmy Florida temperatures, the air was filled with that unmistakable feeling that appears only during the holiday season. The spirit of the season filled the faces of the people he passed on the street, intent on completing their last-minute Christmas shopping. Festivity was everywhere; tinsel hung on the trees, the ubiquitous carols played in department stores and the jolly Santa stand-ins took last-minute requests at the shopping malls. Everything about this time of year brought Rick a tremendous sense of happiness, evoking treasured and joyous memories from a childhood long since left behind.

The sunny days and warm temperatures were a far cry from the chilly winters that Rick had known growing up near Baltimore, Maryland, but even without the winter wonderland, this time of year restored much of that child-like magic in his eyes.

The holiday clock was ticking and, with only three days left until Christmas, Rick knew that he had much left to do. Perhaps that was the part he loved most about this time of year; the hectic pace and hard work gave him such a huge and joyous payoff, it somehow made the long days and short nights enjoyable. While others complained that the season left them exhausted, it served only to energize Rick.

The holidays had been that way for years in the Silanskas house, especially when his children were small. For as long as he had been an adult, Rick divided his holiday time between work, family and church, leaving each one wondering how he had time for anything else.

One of his greatest joys in life was music, and he loved being able to use his talents. During the course of the years, he had begun working at his church, creating spectacular Christmas programs that left people talking for months and wondering how he would out-do himself next time.

Personally, the programs were a time-consuming venture, one that required most of his attention in the hours just before Christmas. Rick would stay late at the church the night before Christmas Eve, going through final rehearsals and making sure that the program was perfect from the first note to the last.

Once the musical production met Rick's satisfaction, he would hurry home to his wife, and they would stay up late into the evening, working together to make the Christmas celebration at home as magical for his own children as the productions at church were for all who attended. They would wrap presents and assemble toys, while Rick would then go back to tinkering with the perfection of his own church presentations, making small changes until the last possible moment.

Even when he and his wife, Stephanie, didn't have the money to indulge their children, there was always plenty of love. That, he had learned long ago, was the greatest gift his children would ever receive.

It was, in many ways, merely an extension of the way he had grown up.

He had been raised in a home that was filled with love, and his earliest memories of Christmas had set the stage for the pleasant years of celebrations that would follow. This remained his favorite time of year, even though now he himself was an adult and two of his four children were on the verge of adulthood themselves. Everything about the season – the celebrations, the traditions and all that accompanies Christmas – never failed to fill Rick with a joy that seemed only to increase with time. It was as if each year only added to the wellspring of memories, building an ever-expanding and seemingly never-ending tide born both of sentiment and sincerity.

Rick knew that he was a fortunate man and that his life was remarkable, if for no other reason than that he had lived it, in its entirety, in love. The son of an Italian mother and a Lithuanian father, he had grown up surrounded by family, laughter, love and music, and all four of those elements continued to be a driving force throughout his adult life. Raised with a deep sense of faith, he had, in recent years, re-evaluated his own beliefs and emerged more steadfast because of that experience.

Perhaps it was because of that renewed commitment that this year seemed so full of possibilities and potential. His business continued to thrive, even as he took a sabbatical from life onstage as a pianist.

This was the time of his life that he had worked so hard for, and he knew that this Christmas, in many ways, marked a turning point in their personal family history. With both Maria and Tony, their two oldest children, away at college, he and Stephanie already were beginning to feel the mixed emotions of seeing a family grow up.

They were proud of the family they had raised, and pleased to see Maria and Tony working so hard to fulfill their own dreams. The future was now in their hands, and as Maria continued her studies to become a teacher, Tony was following closer to his father's career path, completing his education in film. He would soon graduate and join Rick at his company, DreamVision Studios, as director of film projects.

He was pleased that Tony had chosen a career that would allow them to continue their close-knit relationship. DreamVision already was primarily a family effort, with his father serving as senior vice president and brother Vince and his wife, Cris, working alongside him on productions. With togetherness abounding, they even joked at times that the family spent too much time together. Even after the workday had ended, there were children's dance and piano recitals, basketball games, birthday parties and school plays that kept them tethered closer than most families.

Whether the familial closeness came from Italian genes or simply was what many would consider a stroke of good luck was impossible to determine. Rick knew his family was exceptional; while they had their problems and disagreements, there was a tremendous amount of love and concern among them. As the oldest, Rick shared not only an extraordinarily close bond with his mother, but also a protective feeling toward his sister, Dianne, and their younger brother, Vince. Although they were grown now, each with families of their own, the siblings had maintained a closeness that too often fades with time and obligations.

And Christmas, above all other times of the year, served as a reminder of the many blessings that had enriched Rick's life.

As 2002 neared its end, he could look back at the year's events and say that he was, indeed, a fortunate man.

He was looking forward to this season, as always, and looking forward to all that lay beyond it.

Christmas Eve fell on a Tuesday this year, which meant a very short week for him. He was happy to enjoy a slow and uneventful Sunday night before the most hectic part of the holidays kicked in. On Monday, he would shut down DreamVision Studios for the holidays. Meanwhile, Tony and Vince would begin setting up equipment for the Christmas Eve church production. While closing down the studios, Rick would wrap the presents he'd bought for his family, then meet Tony and Vince at the church in the evening. It would be a late night, he knew, but it was a night that was well worth the effort. They would perfect the most minute details of their production, getting it ready for the crowds that would fill the church on Christmas Eve.

He loved watching people leave the church after the Christmas Eve service, filled with the wonder of the season and empowered with the message they had just received. His fascination with snow led him to give one parting gift to the parishioners as they left the service; with the help of six snow machines and four hurricane fans strategically placed on the church's roof, he and Tony created a blizzard of northeastern proportions. It provided a magical moment for everyone, and Rick could never be sure if the joy he felt came from watching the surprise and delight on the people's faces, or if it came simply from being able to enjoy his annual holiday snowstorm.

This year, as he relaxed on that quiet Sunday evening with Stephanie, he contemplated how different it was from the early years of their marriage. Soon, the house would be empty of children and only he and his wife would be left. They had already begun to plan the ways they would spend their time. Jamaica was high on their list, and Rick knew that after years of raising the children and nurturing the household, Stephanie looked forward to time together with him. He had always been aware of how much Stephanie gave of herself; she was the glue that held the family together and the strength behind Rick's dreams.

As much as he loved his children, and treasured the memories of them as small children, Rick was equally thrilled to see them growing into young adults. This would be their time together, he had promised Stephanie. This would be the time they had dreamed of. Yes, they had enjoyed every moment of raising their family together, and there had been plenty of romantic and restful getaways shared only by the two of them. But now it would be different; the years to come would return them to the days of their youth, when their greatest consideration every day was each other, and not kids' schedules, carpools and teenage crises.

He had loved her from the moment he first laid eyes on her, and the idea of having time to be alone with her again left him as excited today as it had more than twenty years earlier.

The house already sported all the trappings of Christmas, and it was an extravagant spread. Rick's passion for this time of year was reflected in the impressively large tree that filled the living room and in the presents that spilled out from beneath it. This would be a good Christmas, he knew it, and he marveled again at the richness of his life.

After wrapping a few Christmas presents, and making a few more notes on the Christmas production, he called it a night, knowing this would be his last chance to get a good night's rest until the holidays were over.

As he sank into a peaceful sleep, he drifted into a world that was waiting anxiously for his arrival. He was entering a dream-like state, but he would never feel as if he were in a dream. Instead, it was as if time and space had been suspended, and he suddenly was ushered into another dimension.

Suddenly Rick was standing at the top of a very old and decaying staircase. As his eyes adjusted to the dim light, it was obvious to him that the rest of his surroundings had not fared much better. He realized he was descending into some sort of basement or cellar, but nothing about this setting held any familiarity or meaning to him. The musty air added to Rick's sense that he was in an old, dusty building that was crumbling from fatigue and dying of neglect.

Curious and eager to discover where he was, Rick turned his attention to the disintegrating walls. It seemed a miracle that they were still standing at all; made of large stones and rocks, and patched together with mortar that had long since seen its better days, there was little left to protect the building from the outside elements.

He realized he was not alone on the steps, but was sharing them with three men whom he did not recognize. The faces were unclear to him, but deep in his heart he knew that they knew him well. It seemed an odd disparity, as he sensed that despite their familiarity with him, he did not know them at all.

As he looked around, he turned his attention to a cavernous area where a hole had been ripped through the wall. It appeared to Rick as if the wall had been blown away by a bomb, and what made him more curious was that there seemed to be a glow of red light coming from somewhere inside that cavernous area.

The three men beside him also turned their attention toward the glowing, gaping hole, and as Rick stood there, transfixed on the light, a little child's body appeared. About half of the tiny child emerged from the area, staring up at the men, silently pleading for help. As she disappeared, Rick gasped and looked at the man on his right, who was non-chalantly drinking a glass of iced tea.

"We have to go help her," Rick said, dumbfounded that none of the men seemed the least bit concerned about the child's welfare.

"Oh, you don't want to go down there," said the man to his right as he stopped Rick before he could make his descent. Rick looked at him, puzzled, unsure of why his mission was being interrupted.

"You don't want anything to do with that," the man continued, and Rick found himself fascinated by the simple fact that the man was holding a glass of iced tea. It seemed oddly out of place in this setting, and Rick fixated on the ice as it swirled in the man's glass. "That's nothing but aggravation. You don't want any part of it."

Anger weighed heavily in the man's voice, and Rick was stunned by the man's callousness. How could they not help that child? How could they not immediately rush to the aid of this tiny, helpless little girl who so clearly needed them? She obviously had been through something horrific and was in danger. How could they turn their backs on her?

Rick felt his anger growing rapidly. He didn't understand how anyone could forsake a little child hiding in this decrepit building. Shaking off the man's admonition to abandon his investigation, Rick pulled away and continued down the stairs.

The floor was made of dirt and as his feet touched it, he wondered whether the building's decrepit condition was caused by age or by outside forces. It was in horrible condition, and he feared for the safety of this child he had glimpsed. Rick walked slowly to where he had first seen her, and she emerged cautiously from behind the rubble. Her eyes were filled with sadness as she stood there, looking up at him.

"She's so tiny!" he exclaimed to himself, amazed that a child could be so small and be obviously alone. Something in his head told him that she was about two and a half years old, but his years of parenting told him she was much too small for that age. She stepped forward, and as his eyes focused on her, Rick's heart melted.

Looking at him with enormous eyes that already had seen too much of the world's unkind side, she didn't say a word but seemed to be crying out for his help. Her light brown hair was unkempt, and her bangs had an unusual part that could have been caused either by a cowlick or an unsteady pair of scissors.

She was obviously scared, and her fear seemed inconsistent with the whimsical little blue jumper she wore, which sported tiny circus animals on each of its two pockets. Even in the poorly lit basement, Rick could see her terror as she reached out her little arms in the air, begging to be picked up. He immediately picked her up and hugged her close to him. He felt as if he could not get close enough to her.

As she wrapped her tiny arms around his neck, Rick sensed that this little girl felt safe for the first time in her short life, and he assured her that she would always be safe with him. She felt as if she had been made to fit perfectly in his arms, and he wondered why he hadn't known sooner that she was waiting to fill a void he did not know existed.

With the little girl now safe in his arms, Rick knew it was time to leave and he turned back toward the stairs. The men who had been so intent on stopping him had disappeared, and as he gazed up at the top of the stairs he saw Stephanie standing there.

As always, she was right there when he needed her and Rick breathed a sigh of relief. He held the child closer to his chest and climbed the stairs. As he reached the top, he carefully extended his arms to pass the little girl into Stephanie's waiting arms.

Rick awoke with a start and was stunned to find his arms empty. He realized he was sobbing, and his pillow had become wet with tears. The ache in his heart matched the emptiness of his arms and he turned to Stephanie, who lay sleeping in the bed next to him. His mind told him this was just a dream, but the piercing pain in his heart told him it was something more. Instead, he felt as if his own child had been stolen from his arms and he knew that he must find a way to get her back.

Slipping quietly out of bed, Rick left his wife's side and made his way to the kitchen. Pouring a tall glass of water, he tried to fight the panic that was rising in his chest.

"This is crazy," he thought. "That had to be a dream. Just a dream."

However, the notion that he dreamed the whole thing made it all the more preposterous to him. While many might have accused him of being a dreamer in the waking world, he was one of those who rarely, if ever, remembered what occurred after he left the waking world. He could count on one hand all of the dreams he had even remembered after he woke. It wasn't at all like his younger daughter, Jessica, who dreamed creative works of art in vivid Technicolor and seemed to have a director working overtime to orchestrate her night-time productions. Rick often had marveled at her abilities, not just to capture so much information during the course of one dream, but to remember it after the fact.

Reasoning with himself that the feelings would eventually fade, he tried to shake the thoughts from his head. The clock told Rick it was past three a.m. and he knew he had to get some sleep to prepare himself for the long three days ahead. But deep inside he felt a sense of restlessness and anxiety inside that was beyond anything he had ever known before.

"There has to be a reason for this," he told himself. "Just go back to sleep. You'll be fine."

Finally convincing himself, Rick finished his water and returned to his bed. He felt taxed and overwhelmed by the emotional residue of the dream, but as he prayed for peace and sleep, his wish was, mercifully, granted.

As sleep swept over his body, he entered a dream state for the second time that night. This time, his journey began with him waking up in his own bed. It was morning, and a brilliant burst of daylight was shining in his bedroom. His heart was filled with the kind of joy usually reserved for a child on Christmas morning, and he felt as if he would burst with excitement.

Turning to share his buoyancy with Stephanie, he found her side of the bed empty. He pulled back the covers and leapt from the bed, not sure what he would find but certain that a magnificent surprise awaited.

In the kitchen, he found Stephanie and his parents sitting at the table, drinking coffee. As he entered the room, all three of them turned to smile at him and though no words were exchanged, the air was filled with a sense of rapture. Rick could feel the emotion swelling within him and knew what he needed to do next.

Racing up the stairs to the bedrooms where his children slept, he instinctively knew exactly which door to open. Excitement filled his heart as his hand turned the knob and pushed the door ajar.

She was lying there, sleeping peacefully, as beautiful as she had been in his previous dream. It was the exact same child that he had held in his arms earlier, and he studied her perfect, beautiful little face. He noticed that her lips had the tiniest pout to them, created by the fact that her bottom lip was much fuller than the top. Rick was flooded with relief and joy as he watched her, knowing that his daughter was home safe. He marveled at her beauty and innocence, pausing for a moment to silently drink her in with his eyes. Rick's body relaxed with a sigh of contentment as a smile played across his face.

Reality once more jarred him from his dream, and Rick abruptly found himself back in his own bed, Stephanie still sleeping soundly beside him. The joy that had encompassed him just seconds earlier was immediately replaced with a sense of grief and loss. His heart turned to lead, and he once more felt the deep distress that had sidelined him in the wee hours of the morning.

The clock told him it was seven o'clock, time to start the new day. Exhausted both physically and emotionally, Rick crawled out of the bed, being careful not to wake his wife. There weren't many days that she was able to sleep in, but since the children did not have to go to school today, Stephanie could actually get a bit of rest. Rick, mindful of that fact, made his way to the shower as quietly as he could, still feeling stunned and weary from the vivid dreams he had just experienced.

Standing under the hot spray of water, he felt hot tears mingling with the shower's steady stream. Devastated in a way that he could not explain, he was puzzled from the experience and troubled by what it could mean. In his heart, he felt that he had truly experienced the events he had just witnessed in his dream, but he struggled to make sense of it.

It felt as though Rick had suddenly discovered a child that he never knew he had. Instead of fading as the routine of the morning kicked in, the emotions of the dream continued to intensify and he found himself gulping back waves of pain. The little girl's face was etched in his mind, and the memory of her tiny, frail body in his arms was still tangible. Each thought of her brought a fresh wave of pain and longing, and the sobs that racked his body paled in comparison to the ache that gripped at his heart.

To Rick, there was only one possible course of action before him: He had to find the little girl in his dream. Even in his own head, the idea sounded far-fetched, but in his heart the idea made sense. If he could find her in his sleep, perhaps she was waiting to be found. He knew she was out there, knew that she was waiting for him – he just didn't know who or where she was.

He went through the required motions of getting ready for work and walked to the side of the bed, where Stephanie still lay sleeping. He stood there, watching her sleep, wanting to talk to her but not wanting to disturb her rest.

She had been his best friend and confidante for so many years now, and he knew that if anyone would hear his story and understand it, it would have to be Stephanie. She had lived through every moment of his adult life with him, had celebrated life's peaks as well as making sense of its valleys. In many ways, she knew him better than he knew himself, and always seemed to be able to help him better navigate life's currents. There wasn't a secret in the world he couldn't tell her, and regardless of how it sounded as the words tumbled out of his mouth, Rick knew that Stephanie could help him make sense of this seemingly senseless experience.

The idea of telling her, however, clashed with the problem of knowing what to say. He didn't know how to tell his wife that he needed her help to find a child they never knew they had. There was no way to explain it logically, but he knew that if anyone could understand him – or help him understand what would happen – it would be his wife.

As he stood there looking down at her, Stephanie became aware, even in her state of slumber, that she was being watched. Having spent the past two decades as a mother, she was accustomed to waking up to seeing a pair of eyes staring at her, waiting for her to wake up. This time, however, the only surprise was that those staring eyes belonged to her husband, not to one of her children.

She opened her eyes and looked at him as if she knew already that something was wrong. Her words echoed that action.

"What's wrong?" she asked Rick before she had even finished opening her eyes. Even in her state of waking, she could tell that he was distressed. His eyes were rimmed in red and showed the strain of both his tears and his lack of sleep; despite the fact that he was freshly showered and dressed, he looked exhausted and defeated.

"What is it?" she asked, as Rick sank onto the side of the bed and began sobbing again. Stephanie never lifted her head from the pillow, but laid there, waiting for him to share his story.

"I had this, this…dream," he said, frustrated with himself for not knowing a more suitable word. Dreams, after all, were figments of the imagination; this had been something real.

Slowly, with Stephanie's encouragement, he recounted the story of entering the decaying and unfamiliar basement, of seeing the child and holding her in his arms. He told about waking up just before he reached the top of the stairs, where she was waiting, and of returning to sleep only to discover the little girl again.

Stephanie lay there in silence, letting Rick share his story uninterrupted as she tried digesting what he was saying. He watched as tears filled her eyes and rolled down the side of her face. It was a moving story, but Stephanie, too, sensed that this was more than just a dream.

She had been with him long enough to know that he was an emotional and excitable man, one who would happily chase a star and not see the obstacles before it. Stephanie had seen him get excited and determined about many things during the course of their marriage, and she had learned not to speak too soon, but rather to let things play themselves out.

As he spoke of finding this child, Stephanie had her own thoughts on the dream. It was no secret that both of Rick's siblings had designated Rick and Stephanie as guardians for their children in the event that was needed, and there were others who had indicated they wanted their children raised by Rick and Stephanie if something should happen to them. Listening to Rick's story, Stephanie felt certain that they would soon have another child joining their brood, and believed that God probably was preparing them for that child's arrival. In her mind, however, that child was one they already knew, the offspring of a friend or a relative.

Not mentioning her interpretation to Rick, she turned her attention back to his words.

"I know that this doesn't sound right," he said. "But I know that that little girl exists. She's in trouble and we've got to find her. I know where she is, but I don't know how to get to her. She's in Russia."

Even Rick was surprised as the words came out of his mouth. He didn't know where the idea of Russia had come from; he only knew that it made sense, even as he heard it for the first time coming from his own mouth.

Perhaps, Stephanie thought, he was unearthing some long-hidden concern for the orphans in Romania that had been brought to light in the early nineties. She remembered seeing news reports and documentaries of starving, abused and disabled Romanian orphans, and wondered if somehow that had translated in Rick's sleeping mind to a single child that he somehow believed to be in Russia. She had no way of knowing at the time that such information had never found its way to Rick, who was startled to learn of the plight of those orphans when it finally was brought up in conversation. He had, in fact, spent much of his adult life either in a recording studio or at a piano, letting the events of the world play out as he happily created music. They had never discussed Russia and certainly had not contemplated adding another child to their house, despite the repeated requests from their youngest child, Andrew, who desperately wanted a younger brother or sister.

Regardless of what had prompted the dream, Stephanie knew that whatever had taken place during the course of the night had deeply concerned Rick and left him troubled and inconsolable. She took his hand, knowing there was little that she could say or do to comfort him at that moment.

"Let's just pray about this," she said. "Let's just ask for guidance."

They held hands and as Rick wept, they asked for God's wisdom. Throughout the course of their marriage, Stephanie had seen her husband become emotional and excitable over many different things, but she had never seen him quite like this. She knew there was something different about this time, but was not sure what it was. Ever the pragmatist, she wasn't going to try to assign a meaning to these events just yet. Instead, Stephanie acknowledged that they were probably being prepared for something new to occur in their lives. Knowing it was out of their hands, she squeezed Rick's hand, wishing him encouragement for the day and telling him that everything would be all right. He looked unconvinced, his eyes filled with a sorrow and distress that even Stephanie could not understand.

They moved slowly through the morning, with Rick taking his time. He was having trouble pulling himself together and he was in no hurry to get the day's events started. Somehow, his energy and enthusiasm, which usually seemed limitless during the holidays, was gone.

As she watched him leave the house, she realized that the weight upon his heart was almost more than he could bear, and she silently wondered what it all meant. She knew something powerful was happening, but also knew that it was something only time and God would reveal.

Chapter Two

The morning sun streaming through his car windows could do nothing to lift Rick's somber mood. What usually was one of the happiest days of his year suddenly seemed to have lost all meaning and fascination.

Commandeering the family van to the warehouse where he had hidden the Christmas presents he'd bought for his wife and children, his mind no longer was filled with his usual sense of holiday excitement. It was as if someone had entered his world as he slept and created a different reality for him; the world that he had known just twenty-four hours earlier seemed to have disappeared.

For years, Rick's own personal holiday tradition had involved buying Christmas presents and keeping them hidden from his children until Christmas morning. These days, he kept his purchases stored in a warehouse and would spend the day before Christmas Eve wrapping presents and writing notes to accompany the gifts. He would then sneak them back to the house and keep them stored in his van until all the children were in bed on Christmas Eve.

It was one more part of the holidays that he adored. As he wrapped gifts, he listened to Christmas music, lost in the wonderment of the moment and filled with appreciation for the many gifts he had been blessed with throughout his life. This year, however, the joy that typically accompanied his gift-wrapping ritual was absent, and the warehouse felt cold and empty. Even the holiday music could do nothing to put him in the spirit of the season. As he wrapped his gifts, everything about his actions suddenly seemed unimportant and irrelevant.

Somewhere, he knew, she was out there. The thought of the little girl he had held in his arms during the night broke his heart each time she entered his mind. He was haunted by her scared little face, and the fear and loneliness inside those wide brown eyes penetrated to the center of his soul. Each thought of her crashed like a wave through his entire body, piercing him with a kind of grief and pain he had never known existed.

Looking around the warehouse at the brightly wrapped presents, he wished he could just put the holidays on hold, just stop the tape from playing, stop the music, stop the noise. He wanted only to find his missing child, and knew that, instead, he must concentrate on the celebrations that would fill the next two days.

Rick folded down the back seat of the van and loaded his freshly wrapped gifts into it. Part of him felt guilty for not having gotten anything for the little girl, and he felt horrible that she would not get any presents from him this year. The thought of her spending Christmas away from him was overwhelming. He once again wiped away the tears that he had been spilling all day, and finished loading the presents into the van.

As he drove to his office in Orlando, he called Stephanie.

"This isn't going away," he told her, and she could hear the desperation in his voice. She listened to him, letting him talk and cry, partly not wanting to interrupt him and partly not knowing what to say. Stephanie knew something dramatic was happening to her husband, and had known it from the moment she had opened her eyes that morning. But what, exactly, was happening remained a mystery that she was unable to comprehend; nor could she find a way to comfort him.

Instead, she gently encouraged him to just get through what he needed to get done and then come home. Stephanie's compassion was the closest thing to comfort that he could find at that moment. They would figure this out together, she assured him, and he wanted so desperately to believe her.

Everything inside of Rick was shifting, and he was unable to stop it. The plans he had made for his life had become irrelevant in the course of just one night, and he felt as if he was losing control of not just his life, but his mind and emotions as well.

"You've got to hold it together," Stephanie reminded him. "Let's just get through the next couple of days and then we'll figure this out."

He made his way to his office, which was deserted for the holidays. No one would return to work until after the new year, and as he shut down the office for the coming days, Rick was completely preoccupied with visions of the little girl. His body convulsed in pain at the thought of her disappearing from his arms, and each time he closed his eyes, he could see that innocent face. The pain and frustration was too great, and Rick sat alone in his office and released deep, body-shaking sobs that threatened to break his heart.

It was, once again, Stephanie who provided him with the strength and encouragement he needed. As she hung up the phone, she sensed that the pain he was experiencing would not soon disappear. She knew from years of experience that when Rick set his sights on something, he pursued it one hundred percent and simply could not be distracted from his goal. Knowing he would not let go of this dream, she had told him instead just to put it aside and get through the holidays. This would give them time to think, Stephanie reasoned, and perhaps the answer to this intensely puzzling question would come to them.

At his office in Orlando, nearly an hour away, Rick could not have felt farther removed from Stephanie's pragmatic optimism. He had no idea how he could get through the next couple of days or even the next couple of hours. All he knew was that he had no choice in the matter.

Rick returned home, spending most of the drive fighting waves of grief and loss that usually were accompanied by tears. All of the accoutrements of the seasonal celebration were in place; the scented candles were burning, the tree was trimmed and brightly lit, and the house was filled with holiday music. Walking through the door of the Silanskas house during this time of the year was like walking onto the set of a holiday movie; it was nothing short of magical. But

Rick felt none of that as he returned home that afternoon; he felt only a sense of emotional exhaustion and a rising panic to find his lost little girl.

At the church that evening, Vince and Tony already had preparations well under way. They handled the technical aspects of the production and as Rick ran through the musical part of the program, he felt separated from his body. It was as if he was watching himself go through the motions of holiday preparation. He could see himself talking with Vince and Tony about what needed to be done, sharing small talk that now had absolutely no meaning to him.

He had always loved that special feeling of being in the church and preparing for the service. Tonight, however, it was different. His preoccupation with the little girl kept him from enjoying his surroundings, and he kept re-living the moment he had held her in his arms. This feeling was here to stay, he knew, and he found himself fearful of what the night's sleep would bring. He continued seeing her face each time he closed his eyes; he had no idea what might lay in store for him once he went to bed. It felt almost like Ebenezer Scrooge in "A Christmas Carol," who found himself visited by three ghosts on Christmas Eve. Only this time, Rick knew, the answers would not be found so simply. He prayed for that sort of luxury, to go to sleep and discover the clues that would solve this intense puzzle. But deep inside his heavy heart, he knew that wouldn't be the case.

The practice went smoothly enough and Rick returned home, where he and Stephanie shared yet another of their holiday traditions. Each year, his mother bought a fruitcake for them that Rick loved. It was far from your run-of-the-mill fruitcake that has become the butt of holiday jokes; this particular cake came from the world-renowned Georgia Fruit Cake Company, and Rick absolutely savored it. Eating the succulent fruit-laden treat had become part of the annual festivities through the years, and as he and Stephanie sat at the table, the night seemed as normal as it could get.

Rick went to bed reluctantly that night, still stinging from the pain of the night before and feeling as if his anxiety over the situation was escalating instead of getting better. He didn't know what would happen as he tried to get some rest for the day ahead, and although he slept restlessly, he was pleasantly surprised that there were no more dreams waiting for him.

Still, it was not as if the little girl had disappeared. He could see her face when he closed his eyes and the hollow ache in his arms made it feel as if she had physically been pried out of them. Rick prayed for relief, prayed for guidance, prayed for wisdom. And even as he prayed, he was aware that he didn't have any of the answers he needed, and he didn't have the slightest idea of where or how to find those answers.

Christmas Eve dawned with the kind of perfection that is usually reserved for movies and television specials. Years of well-orchestrated holiday planning had made the unfolding of Christmas Eve a special day in the Silanskas house from the moment it began until it finally ended in the wee hours of the next day. Every room reflected the holiday, and the massive, well-decorated tree in the family room stood proudly over a mountain of gifts that later would be joined by the ones hidden in the van. The VCR was fed a steady diet of classic Christmas movies, from "It's a Wonderful Life" and "White Christmas" to the animated favorites "Rudolph, the Red-Nosed Reindeer" and "Santa Claus Is Coming to Town," which Rick had loved since childhood.

In the kitchen, the smell of Santa's White Christmas coffee filled the air. It was a special mix that Rick bought from Barnie's every year, and he always made sure that there was a fresh pot on for him and Stephanie. It was just one of the traditions that had become a part of a joyous occasion, and he loved each moment of days like this. Christmas Eve was the day he always wanted to have last forever, and he savored every moment of it like it was the last piece of Christmas candy.

This year, he wanted only for it all to be over. He watched the colorful lights on the tree, saw the festive paper adorning the gifts, heard the familiar lines from the cache of classic Christmas films. All of them suddenly seemed meaningless, and he just wished he could make it all go away. How can the world be so happy, he wondered, when my child is missing?

Stephanie already had talked to him about keeping his dreams – and the internal struggle that followed – to themselves. She did not want the children to know about it, didn't want their holidays to be thrown into the turmoil that Rick already was embroiled in. He knew she was right, but also knew that keeping it together – and keeping quiet – would be a tremendous struggle. It would take everything he had to keep himself from falling apart, and given the emotional roller coaster he had ridden in the past twenty-four hours, he wasn't sure exactly how much strength he had left.

Deferring to Stephanie's strength, he stayed quiet much of the day, going through the motions of the holiday but feeling drained and hollow inside. He would feel himself slipping at times, and Stephanie's eye would catch his glance. Her look was warm but firm: Keep it together; she seemed to be telling him. Hang in there. We will get through this!

By the time he reached the church for the Christmas Eve mass, Rick had no idea how he had made it through the day – or how he would get through the night.

Sitting in the church that night, Rick barely heard the familiar Christmas message. He played a significant role in the Christmas Eve mass, and singing the songs that he loved so much now seemed like an insurmountable challenge. It was all he could do to make it through the songs without breaking down and weeping, and between numbers he found himself gazing up at the cross.

"Please, Lord," he prayed. "Show me how to find that child. I know she's out there. Please help me find her!"

He could feel the urgency swelling within him, could feel the devastation of his loss growing more insistent with each breath. Rick wanted a Christmas miracle, wanted desperately just to know what was happening inside of him and, most importantly, wanted to reunite with the little girl he had held the night before. Tears streamed down his face as he gazed up at the cross, waiting for an answer that would not come in time for Christmas.

Walking out into the Florida night, the snowstorm he and Tony and Vince had made was in full swing. It never failed to delight the congregation, who danced and played in the fake snow like little children. Rick watched them in silence, politely shaking hands and accepting compliments for his part in the church service. It broke his heart to watch the little children playing in the "snow," and he wished his own little girl could join them.

By the time he returned home, Christmas Eve had slipped into the wee hours of Christmas Day. With the children finally in bed, Rick walked outside to retrieve the presents he had wrapped and stashed in the van the day before. In just a matter of hours, the Florida temperatures had plummeted, bringing a welcome chill that always delighted Rick. He missed the cold weather of his childhood days, and welcomed nights like this when a brisk nip transported him back in time. The timing could not have been more perfect; that sudden chill reminded him of the Christmases he had so enjoyed as a child.

Even though he had grown up in modest surroundings, his parents had always gone out of their way to make the holidays absolutely magical. That feeling of awe for the holidays had remained with Rick throughout his adult life, and he and Stephanie put an incredible amount of effort into making their own children's holidays as special as the ones he had grown up with. The chill in the air seemed to bring all those feelings back to him and, just for a moment, Rick felt comforted. He paused outside of the van, breathing in the brisk air and wondering what was happening to him.

Above him, the stars twinkled brightly and the night sky was clear and beautiful. He gazed up, knowing that God had a perfect plan for his life, but also wondering what all of this could possibly mean. He was a blessed man, by anyone's standards. Born to musical parents who nurtured an appreciation for all forms of music, he had been able to follow his dream from behind the keys of a piano. Rick had made his mark both as a musician and as a businessman, and his DreamVision Studios kept him busy in the television and motion picture business, doing everything from commercials to scoring movies.

All of that had created an affluent and enviable life for Rick, but at that moment he knew that he would gladly trade it all in just to find that little girl. There was, he knew, a reason all of this was happening; he just didn't know what that reason was.

Carrying the gifts from the van inside the house, he and Stephanie continued their holiday routine. They positioned the presents perfectly, so when the children first spied them on Christmas morning, the view would be spectacular. Even though his children were growing up, Rick and Stephanie still left them letters from Santa, and it was their tradition to read out loud the notes Rick had written. Rick once again felt himself becoming detached, as if he was not even a part of what was happening around him. It was as if a glass wall now separated him from the real world, and he watched in silence as he and Stephanie read the notes to one another.

Retiring to bed for a few hours' sleep, Rick was both physically and emotionally exhausted. Stephanie could see that a change had come over her husband in the past two days, but her biggest surprise was that even the holiday celebration – easily his favorite time of the year – could not pull him out of that despondent, heartbroken place.

They prayed together before going to sleep, and Rick's prayers continued into the night. He couldn't stop thinking about his little girl, and the only thing he wanted for Christmas was to hold her in his arms again.

The hustle and bustle of Christmas Day began early in the Silanskas house. As always, the huge stash of presents had the children filled with excitement and anticipation, but the first order of the day was a church service. When the children were small, it seemed that they would burst before being able to open their gifts, but it was a rule that Rick and Stephanie had always abided by: Church first, then gifts.

It was the same way they had chosen to live their lives, putting God first, and knowing that everything else would fall into place after that. Without God, they knew, the nicest home or the best toys in the world meant nothing. And so they began their Christmas by celebrating the true meaning of its day.

Returning home, the excitement of the day always reached a feverish pitch, thanks to the excitement of the children. Rick fed off that kind of elated chaos, and he made as big a production out of opening gifts as he had made of their visual presence under the tree. Playing Santa, he would hand out gifts one at a time, and everyone would wait as each individual gift was opened. It was a special time for the family; no gift was ever too small to be overlooked, and the feeling of togetherness among his family members was overwhelming. Both Rick and Stephanie would be near exhaustion by Christmas morning, but basking in that kind of family love and togetherness always served as an energizing force.

This year, however, was different. Instead of anticipating the marathon parade of presents, Rick dreaded the idea of handing out gifts. His joy was gone and in its place was that hollow ache with which he was becoming so familiar. Going through the motions once again, he handed out the gifts but his mind was on that fifth child, the little girl that he so desperately wanted to see in his arms again. Even as he handed out the presents, he could envision her in his living room. In his mind's eye, he could see her tiny little body tearing open presents with his older children, and it broke his heart to not be able to share that moment with her.

He went through the morning in a daze, completely preoccupied with the missing child. Knowing that his biggest challenge of the day awaited him, he wondered how he would fake his way through the massive family holiday celebration at his parents' home.

His entire family now lived in Florida, and the celebrations at his parents' house were nothing short of breath-taking. For years, Rick and Stephanie had been the only ones with children, but now his sister Dianne and brother Vince had caught up a bit, with each bringing two children of their own into the world. It created a remarkably festive environment, one of joy and excitement that Rick's mother, Carmelita, fueled with her painstaking attention to detail.

She created a holiday blowout that was impossible to replicate but, even in the midst of such massive festivities, Rick and Stephanie knew it was unlikely that his behavior would be overlooked.

"I don't want to go," he told his wife as they prepared for the short afternoon drive to his parent's home. "I can't. It's too much. I just want to stay here with you."

Both of them knew that was impossible; missing Christmas was simply unheard of, particularly in this family.

"You're going to have to go, and you're going to have to keep it together," she told him in a gentle yet firm voice. "Your mother is no fool. She's going to know something's wrong, so you've got to find a way to keep yourself from falling apart over there."

Rick nodded. Stephanie and he had talked about how important it was to keep this matter quiet until they figured out what was going on and what they were going to do about it.

"You can't lay this on your parents," she had already cautioned him. "It's too much. Especially at Christmas. You just can't do it."

Knowing that it was common for Rick and Stephanie to be completely worn out by Christmas afternoon, they decided to use exhaustion as an excuse in case anyone should question Rick's behavior. Stephanie still felt the odds were good that Carmelita would detect something was wrong; she had always shared a special bond with her oldest son and they seemed to have a special kind of insight or intuition into one another's lives. It was not uncommon for them to sense when something was amiss in the other's world, and it wasn't unheard of for one to call the other out of the blue and ask what was wrong – based solely on a "feeling" they'd had.

Still, Stephanie knew they had to give it their best shot, and hoped that the excitement of the children and the hectic nature of the day would help camouflage some of her husband's unusual behavior.

Her hopes were mostly on-target; they arrived with the usual kind of fanfare that can't be avoided when a party of six joins a celebration already under way. Rick greeted his parents with the usual affection, and he once again found himself going through the motions of festivity. Each minute seemed excruciating; it was as if time had been slowed to a snail's pace and he was trapped in some sort of drawn-out production from which there was no escape.

As usual, he and Stephanie sat on a pair of folding chairs in his parents' basement as the gift-giving commenced. The holidays were so filled with tradition that extended down to the last detail, such as the pair of chairs he and Stephanie always sat on. At least during this round of holiday festivity, he was able to defer to his father, who played the role of gift-distributor. It allowed Rick to step out of center stage and instead sit in the wings, and he was grateful for that respite.

The holiday enthusiasm always peaked during his parents' Christmas observance, and the laughter and merriment that filled the room echoed hollow in Rick's ears. As he watched his young nephews happily plowing through their gifts, he could feel the tears welling up in his eyes. He turned to Stephanie and whispered, "I can't do this."

She could see the sorrow in his face, but also knew there was nothing either of them could do about it at that moment.

"Keep it together," she whispered back. "You've got to make it through this."

It all seemed so unfair. The laughter, the lights, the smiles, the food – how could all of these people be so happy when Rick's child was missing? How could they be so light-hearted when she was out there, alone, waiting for him? He marveled at how unjust it seemed for the rest of his family to be able to have all of their children home for the holidays, while his was still lost, missing, waiting for him.

Who was this child? He knew she was his. He knew that from the time her little arms wrapped around his neck. But where was she?

Even as the holiday hoopla continued, Rick felt himself withdrawing more and more into himself as he desperately re-lived his first dream, looking for clues that might help him find her. Just as Stephanie had predicted, his unusual behavior and lack of seasonal gusto did not escape his mother's concerned eye, and she wondered aloud to him if he was feeling all right. As rehearsed, he assured his mother that he was fine and that he was merely tired from the church services.

She continued studying his actions, trying not to let her maternal concern overshadow the holiday but also sensing that something far beyond sleep deprivation was troubling her oldest son. Watching him interact with Stephanie, she could tell that something wasn't right between them.

They had always been best friends, he and Stephanie. From that summer he first met her, it seemed that there was a unique and unbreakable bond between them. Rick was the dreamer, the creative driving force who believed everything was possible. He painted the canvas of his life in broad strokes in brilliant colors; Stephanie was the realist who came in and gave detail and realism to that canvas. Together, it had made for a successful partnership, both romantically and professionally.

Today, however, Carmelita could tell that something had changed for Rick and Stephanie. She did her best to overlook it, but felt a growing concern as the day stretched into night. Perhaps, she told herself, they just had a fight and this will pass. It was, after all, Christmas, and she refused to dwell too long on the possibility that something was amiss.

The entire family was exhausted by the conclusion of Christmas Day, and Rick was relieved to return home and end the day. At the same time, his frustration was growing, and he wished the holidays would magically disappear so he could begin looking for his daughter. He had no idea how he would do that; he only knew that he could not just sit by and pretend that everything was fine.

Once again, Rick found himself both eager to sleep and afraid to return to his bed. Her face would not fade; it seemed only to burn itself deeper into his mind. Lying in bed, he was finally able to release the pain and anxiety that he had kept trapped within him all day, and Stephanie lay there silently beside, listening helplessly as he sobbed himself to sleep.

The pain that greeted Rick the next morning as he awoke was as tangible and formidable as anything he had ever felt. His sense of grief seemed only to be growing, and he knew with certainty that whatever was happening inside of him was not going to diminish with time. The sense that things would return to normal had vanished with the second dream. He realized that the only time he ever felt like this might be just a dream was that moment he stood in the kitchen after waking the first time. Could that really just have been two days ago? He felt like he had lived a lifetime since then, felt as if his grip on reality suddenly had become very tenuous.

The house had emptied, with each of the children eager to share their post-holiday fun with their friends. "I've got to talk to someone," he told Stephanie over coffee. Stephanie looked at him and knew that he needed to take some sort of action; trying to keep this inside was obviously taking its toll on him. He looked rumpled and shaken, his eyes reflecting both the sorrow and exhaustion he felt. She was glad that he was taking steps to resolve this within himself, even as she continued to wonder what, exactly, was happening to him.

Rick had only known Ken Mikesell for about ten months, but already had found a friend he could look to for guidance. Ken was a strong Christian man as well as a trusted confidante, and Rick knew that he could turn to Ken to unleash the burden weighing heavily on his heart. They met for coffee and as Rick poured out his story, Ken listened in silent amazement.

"I know this sounds crazy," Rick said, almost apologetic. "You've got to tell me. Is there something wrong with me?"

Ken found himself immediately moved by the story and had the unmistakable feeling that God's hand had set in motion a powerful series of events. He smiled as Rick pondered his own sanity, a sympathetic smile that came from years of watching God's hand move in powerful ways. He recognized the divine signature authoring this turn of events, and weighed his words carefully as he spoke them.

"Nothing's wrong with you, Rick. God's just moving in your life. All you can do now is just wait and listen."

Nothing seemed more difficult at that moment; Rick felt as if he already had lost too much time waiting. He knew that he needed to take action; he just wasn't sure what it was.

"I have no idea how to find this child, Ken. I know she's in Russia, but I don't know how to find her."

Ken thought of a friend of his who had adopted eighteen children, and he promised Rick that he would get the name of the agency the man and his wife had used. Rick nodded appreciatively, but felt in his heart that he didn't have time to wait for that information. He knew he had to begin his search and, with no other resource available, he returned home and parked himself in front of his computer.

Stephanie could see that his spirits were lifted somewhat; Ken had given him hope and direction, and he now seemed armed to do battle with whatever stood between him and the missing child. She stood over his shoulder, watching as he pulled up his Internet browser and immediately went to the Google search engine.

Rick could feel a sense of anticipation and excitement as he sat there; he was placing so much hope in this search and he felt it was, at that moment, his only opportunity to find peace of mind. He entered "adoption agency" into the search engine, and the results came back with Open Door Adoption Agency. The agency, he saw, was located in Thomasville, Georgia and he made a note of it.

Continuing his search, he decided to refine his information and now typed in "adoption agency Russia." Again, Open Door Adoption Agency's name appeared on the screen.

"I've already got that," he said, to no one in particular, and entered "adoption" into the search engine. As Open Door Adoption Agency's name appeared for a third time, Stephanie patted his shoulder and said, only half-joking, "Do you think you've got the message yet?"

He realized that he was, indeed, being directed toward Open Door, and his hands were trembling as he picked up the phone. He did not know what to expect as he dialed the number, and as the phone kept ringing, his heart sank. It is the day after Christmas, he thought to himself. Of *course* nobody is there! The now-familiar frustration flooded him again.

"It's alright," Stephanie reassured him. "Try them again tomorrow."

Tomorrow seemed a lifetime away; between now and then, he would have to suffer yet another excruciating night of not knowing where his child was. He would have to endure another seemingly endless night of watching those helpless eyes looking at him, begging him to rescue her. He realized that it was likely no one would be in the office the following day, which was a Friday. Then the agency would be closed for the weekend, and since New Year's Eve was the following Tuesday, he wasn't sure if he would be able to reach anyone until after 2003 had begun. It seemed the worst form of torture imaginable, to be so close to finding help, only to be denied. And, as he had done so many times during the past three days, Rick did the only thing he knew to do as he climbed into bed that night: He prayed while the tears streamed down his face.

Chapter Three

The days surrounding the holidays were typically quiet ones for Ed Thomas. While the rest of the working world faced end-of-the-year deadlines and the frenzied but festive chaos that typically accompanies corporate America's last month of the year, Ed found the end of December to be one of the calmest times for him – at least as far as work was concerned.

As the Eastern Europe Program Director for The Open Door Adoption Agency, and from his prior experience with adoptions, Ed knew that the holidays were not usually the time when families made inquiries. With Russian officials enjoying their own holidays, and most American households finding themselves awash in activity, Ed knew he had little to do until the new year began.

Knowing that this was the perfect time to tie up loose ends, Ed decided to take advantage of the slow days preceding the dawn of 2003. It was Friday, December 27, and he already had enjoyed a few days' break because of Christmas; he might as well go into the office and get ready for the coming year, which now was just under a week away.

It came as a surprise when his phone rang, and that surprise would continue to unfold as he picked up the receiver. The instant he said "hello," the words tumbled out from the other end. Ed could do little besides sit there and listen to the story that the man was bursting to tell.

"I hope you don't think I'm crazy," Rick began as soon as he had identified himself. "But I have to tell you about this dream that I had."

As Rick's words spilled from his mouth, Ed felt the combination of sincerity and frustration exploding through the phone. And while the story was highly unusual, the emotion and determination with which Rick spoke told Ed that nothing about this phone call was contrived.

His voice quivering with emotion, Rick told his entire story; he relayed his first dream, where he initially saw the tiny little girl in the basement, and Ed instantly found himself caught up in both the detail and the emotion of the dream. Rick told the story in such excruciating detail that it seemed as if he was re-living it as the words escaped his mouth.

As Rick conveyed the second dream, where he found this very child sleeping in a room in his home, Ed felt a wave of amazement sweep over him. At that very moment, he knew with absolute certainty that the events he saw unfolding were being masterminded by a power far greater than anything human. As a Christian, Ed was aware of the power of faith, but rarely had he seen it so clearly spelled out. It was as if God had reached down and personally handed Rick a specific set of instructions to solve what others might consider an impossible riddle.

It was then that Ed knew without a shadow of a doubt that the tiny girl who Rick so frantically needed to locate was waiting for them. The only real hurdle they needed to clear was the simple task of finding her.

"I don't know why, Ed, but for some reason, I know that little girl is in Russia. It's just a feeling I have."

Rick's words took Ed by surprise. It was only then that he revealed to Rick that he was the person responsible for adoptions in Eastern Europe. The simple fact that he was at his desk when Rick called now seemed to be just one more well-scripted scene in a dramatic play.

"I believe you, Rick. And I think you're right. I can't explain why, but I think we'll find her in Russia."

From his years working with adoptions, Ed knew that the people who called an agency were at a critical point. In most cases, their decision had already been made before they contacted the agency, and Ed held to the philosophy that it was important to give each family the time and respect that accompanies such a weighty decision. He had talked to numerous families, but had never seen or heard someone who had received such a clear and profound directive.

Rick again reiterated to Ed his hopes that he didn't sound completely crazy. Ed laughed and measured his words carefully before he replied.

"I have no doubt that this happened," Ed said, realizing even as he spoke that he was in the center of a miracle that was in its infant stages. "And I have no doubt that we will find her."

They were the words Rick had waited to hear. Even though only four days had passed since he first had his vision of the little girl, he felt as if he had lived a torturous lifetime without her. Ed's words wrapped around his heart like a warm, comforting blanket, and he knew that he had been led to the right man.

Rick turned to Stephanie, who stood beside him as he talked on the phone. He smiled at her, nodding his head and giving her the "thumbs-up" sign. And although they had not actually discussed it, both of them knew what needed to be done next.

"Can you send me every bit of paperwork I need to begin the adoption process?" Rick asked. "I want to get this all done so that when we find her, we can be ready for her."

Even though Rick's faith colored every nuance of his conversation, what Ed found most interesting was that Rick and his wife were chosen, seemingly, from out of the blue. Ed marveled that a couple who had never considered adding to their family was now, in blind faith, proceeding with what appeared to be a clear-cut missive from above. He could tell that Rick was overwhelmed by the events that were playing out in his life, but he also sensed Rick's determination to follow through, and to do so swiftly.

Already, Rick was referring to the little girl as his daughter. He had the concern and grief of a parent whose child was missing, and Ed felt both empathy and amazement as they talked. He explained the process for international adoptions, advising Rick that it would take about sixty days for them to be approved as an adoptive home, and the entire process of international adoptions typically took between three and six months.

Rick's heart fell at the mention of such an extended time frame. He wanted to find her now; he desperately needed to hold her in his arms, have her living in his home, in a matter of days, not months. The thought of enduring another night without her was heart-breaking; to think of not having her in his home for another six months was almost more than he could bear.

As Ed took down Rick's email information, another thought crossed his mind. He had worked with numerous couples who felt they were called to adopt a child from a specific region, but this was the first time he had ever been approached by someone looking for a specific child that they had already seen – particularly one they had seen in a dream.

"Can you provide me with some sort of description or drawing of the child you're looking for? I feel that might be helpful in finding her," Ed requested.

The request resonated through Rick in an unexpected way. It spoke to an irrational fear he had experienced from the time he first became a parent, but had never shared with anyone.

For some reason, from the time his daughter Maria was born, Rick had been shadowed by a fear that, one day, one of his children would be missing and he would be unable to find any current pictures of them. Instead, he would have to sit down with a police sketch artist and try to explain the face he knew so well as precious minutes ticked off the clock. Entire nightmares had been devoted to that topic in his early years as a parent, and now that deep-seated fear seemed to be coming to fruition.

"Absolutely. I'll get right on that," Rick found himself replying. "I'll get that to you as soon as I can."

Both men hung up their respective telephones, profoundly affected by the phone call. Ed firmly believed that God speaks to different people in different ways, and there was no mistaking where this message was coming from. He knew that he had just joined part of an inspired search, and despite how it looked from the outside, he sensed that this would be among the smoothest adoptions he participated in. The hand of God was clearly resting on Rick's shoulder, and it was simply a matter of following where they were led.

Rick felt both relieved and shattered as he put down his telephone. From the moment that Ed had confirmed Rick's feelings that he could find that little girl, Rick had felt his heart lighten for the first time in days. Before he had called Ed, he felt lost and adrift, unsure of where to go for help. Now, he had a plan of action. And he felt he had a guide to accompany he and Stephanie on a journey that was both foreign and unavoidable.

Ed's email with the necessary paperwork arrived almost immediately, and as Rick printed out the pages, it was clear that he had Stephanie had plenty of homework before them. No detail of their lives was overlooked, and the reality of the task at hand seemed enormous. Every document had to be notarized, and it was a massive amount of information to compile. He wanted to get it done immediately, as it seemed as each blank line on those forms stood as one more hurdle between him and the little girl in his dreams.

Rick and Stephanie took the pages to their kitchen table and began filling out the forms. The house was quiet, with the children each enjoying their holiday breaks from school by spending it with friends.

"You know we're going to have to talk to them soon," Stephanie said, noting that they were bound to realize something was unusual was going on. Rick nodded. He wanted to get a little bit further along in the process, and wanted to come to terms with what was happening within him before he tried explaining it to his children. Rick felt buoyed and encouraged by his phone conversation with Ed; he no longer felt as if he and Stephanie were on a covert mission alone.

"He wants me to get a picture or description of her to help him look for her," Rick said, and he already knew where he would turn for that help. "I'm going to call Armando and see if he can meet me tomorrow."

Armando Escalante had worked with Rick on numerous projects in the eight years they had known one another. A skilled artist,

Armando's talent seemed to have no boundaries; he was just as adept at creating a computer-generated animation as he was at painting a life-like portrait or still life. Those talents had served him well, and he was known in the industry as someone who could not only illustrate projects, but was also an accomplished producer and director.

Rick had long been fascinated by Armando's talent, and had marveled at his ability to transform Rick's thoughts and ideas into art. Now, at the time he needed it most, Rick knew that Armando was the one person who could transcribe the images in his mind and put them on paper.

More than a year had passed since they had last seen one another, but Armando was not particularly surprised to hear from Rick. The course of their working relationship was one that saw them working together in close contact for periods of time, then drifting off to work on other projects, knowing they could rely on one another again when time and circumstances called for it. They exchanged pleasantries, and as Rick approached the reason for his phone call, he made his words sound as casual as he knew how.

"I wondered if you had some time to get together," Rick asked, somehow managing to keep the urgency from his voice. "I have a portrait that I'd like you to do."

Sandwiched between the holidays, Armando found himself with some much-welcomed free time on his hands, and instantly agreed to meet with Rick to discuss the project.

Rick could feel the anxiety as he drove to Orlando the next day, fully aware of how important this lunch-time meeting would be. The feelings of urgency only continued swelling within him, and he felt at times that he could not endure another moment of the grief and loneliness within. His prayers continued around the clock, praying for guidance, for peace, and most of all, praying for a way to find that precious little child who so desperately needed his help.

They met at an Olive Garden restaurant in Orlando, about an hour from Armando's Port Orange-based studio. Nothing about Rick's demeanor gave Armando any indication that something was wrong; they settled into their booth and ordered lunch, exchanging small talk about their holidays and catching up on the various projects each was working on. It was only after their lunch had arrived that Rick's conversation took a more serious turn, and he began relating the story of his pre-Christmas dream.

In his years of working with Rick, Armando had come to know him as a fair and sensitive man, someone who followed his heart but only after double-checking that path with God. Although Rick had always been a spiritual man, he now seemed even more steadfast than ever before, and as he told Armando, in excruciating detail, the experience of a few nights earlier, it was clear that he was a man on a mission.

Armando could tell that Rick believed this was much more than a dream, and it left the illustrator uncertain of what to make of it. It was obvious that the experience was not just a dream but a real experience for Rick, and it had made an unshakable impression on him. He was unable to walk away from it, unable to think of much else. Rick had taken this dream as a divine presentation, and now he was determined to move forward. However, he now needed the help of his old friend to make that next step.

"I can see her sitting there, Armando. I can see her as clearly as I can see you sitting in front of me," Rick said. The determination in his eyes was unmistakable.

"But I don't know how else to show her to someone else. I need a picture of her."

Armando pulled out his sketch pad and they began working. It was not the first time that the artist had taken words and shaped them into art, but he had never experienced it quite like this. Usually when clients gave him a description, it was a general idea; when he had painted or drawn portraits from the past, he at least had a photograph to refer to. But the detail with which Rick remembered the child made it easy for him to begin stroking the page with his pencil.

Although many people would later marvel at Rick's attention to detail, Armando didn't find it particularly surprising that this dream remained so vivid in his mind. As a child, Armando had experienced his own vivid dream, one that found him walking down an unfamiliar road in an unidentified countryside. As he walked through the early morning mist, he came upon a little white church overlooking a valley. Even in his sleep, the scene took his breath away and it stayed with him for years, always evoking the same sense of emotion by its beauty. After carrying the image in his head for twenty years, he painted the scene exactly as it had appeared in his sleep and for years afterward that picture hung on a wall in his home.

Rick's dream shared the kind of vivid detail that Armando had known, but whereas Armando's dream had given him a sense of peace, Rick's had shaken him to the core of his soul. As Rick guided Armando with descriptions of the little girl, the distress of his voice became more obvious to Armando. In Rick's mind, this was a life and death situation, and while Armando still wasn't quite sure of what to make of Rick's experience, he could tell that Rick viewed it as a clear-cut call to action.

They passed the sketchpad back and forth, with Armando completing sketch after sketch and Rick suggesting revisions. Much of their focus was on the little girl's mouth, which Rick remembered so clearly. Her top lip was much thinner than her bottom lip, and after several attempts, Armando slid the pad across the table one more time.

Rick's eyes reddened and his face registered complete recognition as he gazed at the drawing.

"That's her!" he exclaimed. "That is the exact child I held in my arms. That is *her*, Armando!"

Even though Rick had every confidence in Armando's ability, he found himself amazed at how well the artist had captured the little girl's likeness on paper. The detail was perfect, right down to the cowlick that created uneven bangs across the child's forehead. Rick looked into the enormous brown eyes and they seemed to jump off the page and physically tug at his heart.

"Can you put some color on it?" he asked, and Armando nodded. He would take it home to his studio, colorize it and then send Rick a digital image by email. Rick gazed at the picture, not wanting to let her out of his sight. Now, he realized with a sigh of

Artist's sketch

relief, he had something to show everyone. No longer was this just someone trapped in his head, crying for help; she was a physical presence that others could see.

"Wonderful job, Armando," he said. "I knew you could do this. Thank you. Thank you so much."

Armando was glad to have helped, and hoped for the best; still, he wasn't sure what to expect next. He could see that Rick was very excited by the drawing, and Armando knew this portrait made her more real to him. Armando looked at her little face and wondered what would happen. If this truly was what Rick had seen in his dream then, yes, Armando felt, he had drawn the little girl. But he was not convinced that she existed and hoped the drawing would, at the very least, give Rick some comfort.

More than four hours had passed when they finally left the restaurant, and Rick's heart felt lighter than it had in days. He was so eager to show Stephanie the portrait, so eager to share this picture with the rest of the world. But most of all, he just wanted to find the little girl who belonged to those sad, searching eyes.

He stopped by his office for a couple of hours and, by the time he arrived home, Armando already had sent a color-enhanced digital image of the drawing. He opened the image and found himself once more overcome with awe. He printed it out and raced back downstairs to show it to Stephanie.

The couple stood there, silently, looking upon the child that they knew they would walk to the ends of the earth to find. It was a quiet moment, one that filled both of them with awe. For Stephanie, it was the first opportunity to see the child that her husband had tried to describe to her in detail. For Rick, it was as if he was looking at a child he knew, a child he had carried in his heart for what already seemed like an eternity.

Stephanie could see that the portrait had affected Rick, and it only served as confirmation of the path they were on.

"We've got to send this to Ed," Rick said. "This is going to do so much to help us find her."

He raced back to his computer and forwarded Armando's drawing to Ed, adding his own personal note. Rick desperately wanted the drawing to prompt immediate action, and wanted so badly for Ed to find this child as soon as he opened the email. Rick knew in his heart that the process was going to take longer than he would like, he just wasn't sure how he would survive such a lengthy chain of events.

At his office in Georgia, Ed noticed the new email as it arrived. He had asked Rick to give him a description in hopes that he would have some sort of aid to help simplify the search. As he opened Rick's email, he was amazed by what he saw.

They had never discussed Rick's profession, and Ed had no idea that Rick had access to resources such as Armando. Ed looked in amazement at the picture, marveling at how detailed it was. He felt a chill run through his body. In all his time of working with potential adoptive families, he had never experienced anything like this. It seemed ordained by God, and he shared Rick's belief that the little girl they sought would be found in Russia. Now, armed with an actual portrait of her, Ed was more convinced than ever that they would find her.

He began emailing the image to his associates in the Ukraine, Russia and Eastern Europe. Ed had no idea how this would unfold, or how long the search would take. But at that moment, he was convinced more than ever that she was waiting for them to find her. All that stood between them was half a world and dozens of orphanages scattered across eleven time zones. While they were, literally, looking for a child that was one in a million, Ed remained convinced that this adoption was simply a matter of time.

With the search for their little girl intensifying, Rick and Stephanie knew it was time to begin telling their families about the changes that they believed would be happening quickly within their home. They agreed to tell the children first, then talk to Rick's parents before telling his brother and sister. Stephanie's family lived in England, and Stephanie knew she could buy a bit more time before talking with them.

"The kids are going to get suspicious before long," Stephanie noted. "We need to tell them soon."

"We have to tell them all at the same time," Rick said, knowing that there was simply no other way to present this to them than as a family.

Maria already had returned to school in Tampa, but Rick and Stephanie had tickets to take the three other children to the theater that weekend. It was the first weekend of the new year, and Rick had purchased tickets to the big-band production, "Swing!" in Melbourne, Florida. That would provide the perfect opportunity to get all the kids in one place and tell them what was about to happen; Stephanie called Maria and asked her to meet them for dinner.

Having already spent most of her Christmas break at home, Maria was eager to resume her own schedule, and resisted the invitation. Stephanie finally convinced her to meet them, unknowingly raising questions in her oldest daughter's mind.

Rick did his best to act as normal as he could manage, but as they waited for the weekend to arrive, he was completely preoccupied with the little girl. He was eager to share the news with his four children, excited to tell them about the little sister they were going to have. Stephanie cautioned him to choose his words carefully, knowing that regardless of how they responded to what their father said, these events were going to turn their current lives upside down.

As they made the two-and-a-half-hour drive to Melbourne, the rest of the world seemed to disappear for Rick. It was becoming almost familiar, this odd sensation of living in a world that he wasn't really a part of. While events went on around him, Rick found himself completely immersed in thoughts of that child. He could see her every time he closed his eyes, could still feel her frail little body in his arms. The sensation of those tiny arms clutching his neck brought tears to his eyes, and each breath felt like a sharp, winter wind blowing through his heart.

In the seat behind him, Tony, Jessica and Andrew laughed and joked the time away. He could picture her back there with them, could see how perfectly that little girl belonged with them. It both comforted and pained him, renewing his determination while at the same time testing his emotional stamina.

Oblivious to what their father was going through, the three younger Silanskas children took their places at the table of the Italian restaurant; moments later, Maria joined them.

She had driven from Tampa to Melbourne alone, and the more than two hours she spent in her car gave her plenty of time to wonder why her mother had been so insistent that she met them. She felt certain that Stephanie would have told her if something was truly wrong, but there was something veiled and mysterious about her mother's determination to include her in the evening.

It was, in many ways, an uneventful dinner; while the children bantered amongst themselves, caught up in the daily details of adolescence and young adulthood, Rick spent most of the meal thinking about the news he was about to deliver. He was bursting to finally share his secret, eager to tell the story he was convinced would change all of their lives forever. Although Stephanie had warned him that it might take the children some time to accept his news, he was convinced they would be as excited as he was.

With dinner completed, Rick looked around the table and cleared his throat.

"We brought all of you here tonight for a very specific reason," he began, and suddenly he felt the emotion welling up within him again. "We have something we have to tell you."

The mood changed instantly and the children exchanged wide-eyed, wondering glances.

"Tell me you're not dying and that grandma and grand-dad are fine," said Maria, blurting out the two biggest fears in her life.

"No, everyone is fine," Stephanie assured the rest of the table. "Your father just has something important he needs to tell you."

It took Rick several minutes to get to the heart of the story, and during his preamble, the hearts and minds of each of his children were racing in different directions. What could he possibly be leading up to? None of the ideas that came to them, individually, even came close to what he was about to tell them.

He slowly went through the story again, re-telling his first, vivid encounter with the little girl in the ramshackle basement. Rick recounted his torturous awakening, the terror of finding his arms empty and his vain attempt to sort out the meaning of the dream before he returned to his bedroom for a second dream. It was obvious to everyone at the table that he had clearly seen something; they just weren't sure what that meant to them.

Everyone who knew Rick was accustomed to seeing him make his ideas become reality simply by setting his mind on his goals. But this, they all knew, was different. He was beyond determined; he was driven in a way that even they had never seen before.

He explained the process they were going through, told them that they were completing the paperwork to get their home approved for adoption and, as soon as that happened, their family would expand to include the little girl he had seen.

As he finished telling his story, he pulled his briefcase from beneath his chair and produced the picture that Armando had drawn.

"You already have her picture?" Tony asked, assuming that meant he and Stephanie already had found the little girl from the dream.

Rick looked at them and shook his head. "No, I had Armando sit down with me and draw this. This is the little girl I saw in the dream. We don't know where she is, but this is the little girl we are going to find and adopt."

A blend of excitement and apprehension filled the hearts of his children. It was an unusual story, no question about that. Still, the determination on their father's face and the unwavering support of their mother made it seem, somehow, almost normal.

Stephanie excused herself to go to the bathroom and wasn't entirely surprised that both of her daughters followed her. Jessica, their younger daughter, seemed somewhat in shock; Maria, as usual, took the role of the concerned eldest child.

"So, what do *you* think of all this?" she asked Stephanie, studying her mother's face carefully for a reaction. "What do you think is happening?"

Stephanie had spent the last ten days living with this, mulling over what her husband had seen and trying to make sense of this unexpected turn of events.

"I don't know," she told her daughters, giving them the only honest answer she could. "I know that your father saw something, and I know that something is going on here – but I can't tell you what it is. It's something we just have to go through and wait and see what God has for us."

It was not the definitive answer the girls had hoped their mother could provide, and they continued to press her for details.

"This is kind of out there," Jessica observed. "Even for dad – it doesn't make sense."

Stephanie already had come to accept what was happening to them, and that lesson now was something the rest of the family would learn as well. This wasn't an event in the family history that could be neatly defined and categorized; unlike births and weddings and deaths and other major family milestones, this one came without any sense of reason or familiarity. It had burst upon them, a surprise that they had not chosen with a plan they were not privy to.

It was faith, pure and simple. Stephanie and Rick had raised their children with the strong spiritual foundation that they both made central in their lives, but nothing in either Rick or Stephanie's past had called for this kind of faith. Now that the children had heard the story, they were joining their parents on a remarkable journey, one that would not let them depend upon the physical world. Instead, they would learn to believe in what could be and watch as it materialized into what would be.

She knew that there was little she could say to slow the spinning minds of her children at this point. The best she could do was be open and honest with them, answering questions the best she could as they settled into the idea of the new adventure they were unwittingly now a part of.

Stephanie would watch them over the next few days and weeks, bearing witness to their growing ease with the idea of adding a young sister to the mix. She correctly suspected that Andrew would be the most comfortable with the idea; for years their youngest child had asked why he didn't have a little brother or sister. That request was about to be answered, Stephanie could feel it, although she could not yet explain it to anyone else.

She had decided to wait to tell her own family about the latest turn of events. As a family full of accountants and insurance salesmen in England, Stephanie's life with a creative, musical husband always had seemed rather foreign to them. They marveled at his latest projects but always seemed just a bit skeptical; she knew that this news would simply be too much for them.

Instead, it was time to begin telling Rick's family. She had married into a dramatic family, but she strongly suspected that this might be overpowering, even for them. Still, despite how overwhelming it might seem, she also knew they would be as supportive of this as they had been with everything Rick had attempted and accomplished in his life. It was partly because of that support that Rick had always believed he could do anything. He never saw obstacles, only the goals that lay beyond them.

"Why did this happen to me?" Rick had asked Stephanie one night, shortly after the dream had taken place.

"Because you'll do something about it."

She knew that was true, and believed with all her heart that God had chosen her husband to follow Him on a wonderful journey. But where that would take them now became a matter of blind, devoted faith. When Rick first had related his dream to her, she knew he was being called for some mission, but thought the child was merely a symbol of those needing their help. To be honest, Stephanie had expected his intensity to wane as the days passed, but instead his sense of passion and urgency only seemed to multiply with each passing day.

Stephanie felt like she had been swept up in a tidal wave, and she now was caught up in something that seemed to grow more powerful each day. The best that any of them could do was to hold on and believe that each day would bring them one step closer to an answer.

Chapter Four

Now that Rick and Stephanie had shared with their children the unusual turn of events taking place, they turned their attention to Rick's immediate family. Rick knew from experience that they would be supportive, even though others might be skeptical about what he had to say.

His family had always been there for him wholeheartedly. And now, when he needed their love and understanding more than ever before, he had no doubts that they would be there for him.

It was a given that he would tell his parents first. He also knew that he wanted to share the news with Dianne and Vince, his younger sister and brother, as close to the same time as possible. Rick and Stephanie were sensitive to the fact that his news would travel quickly among family members, and he didn't want anyone to feel left out of a very important loop. The first phone call went to his parents, who agreed to meet Rick and Stephanie for dinner.

Richard and Carmelita Silanskas had watched their oldest son's achievements with pride and amazement. In their eyes, there was no such thing as failure, only plans that did not work out quite the way one first envisioned them. Through the years, they had watched as Rick took many different avenues to make his musical career more successful, and the results had been varied. The consistent theme through all of those attempts, however, had been his parents' unwavering pride and support.

They had no doubts that their son's ability on the piano would one day propel him to lofty heights, even beyond his career ambitions. But it was the man Rick had become that they were most proud of.

Even as a child, Rick had exhibited extreme compassion and concern for others. He was exceptionally close with his mother, now enjoying a bond originally born of adversity. Rick was just three months old when his dad was stricken with tuberculosis, forcing Richard into a hospital for more than a year. It was a difficult time for Carmelita, who balanced visiting her husband in the hospital with caring for her infant son. Although it created a hardship for her, it also spawned a lasting and unbreakable bond between mother and son. Throughout his life, Rick had given special care and attention to his mother, and Carmelita never ceased to be amazed at the continued selflessness of her oldest son.

His telephone call came out of the blue; a simple request to meet for dinner. In the past, such calls, in which Rick almost sounded too nonchalant, as if he was working at hiding a secret, generally meant that Stephanie was pregnant. Carmelita rolled the idea around in her head. Could it be? At forty-three, it wasn't out of the question for Stephanie, but Carmelita could not imagine them having another child. With both Maria and Tony in college, and Jessica and Andrew in their teen years, it was unfathomable that Rick and Stephanie would want to continue adding to their brood. Carmelita pushed that thought from her mind.

Still, it was obvious that something was up, and if it wasn't a pregnancy, Carmelita feared it might be something far less joyous. She wondered if one of them were sick, wondered if this beautiful family portrait they had painted through years of love, hard work and faith was about to be shadowed by a darker hue.

Richard and Carmelita were the first to arrive at Picadilly Cafeteria, inside the Lake Square Mall in Leesburg, Florida. Carmelita was unsure if it was anxiety or anticipation that she felt; most of all, she just wanted to know what the mystery was behind this meeting. The few minutes' wait for Rick and Stephanie gave her the chance to mentally examine possible causes for this gathering, and she was relieved when they finally appeared at the table. The family's matriarch barely gave them time to sit down before turning to Stephanie and looking her in the eye.

"Don't tell me you're pregnant..." she began, and Rick and Stephanie exchanged a look.

"Well, not *exactly*," Stephanie said, not certain how the conversation should proceed. She deferred to Rick, who turned to his parents with an earnestness that caught the immediate attention of the older couple.

"Mom, Dad, I have something to tell you, but I don't want you to get upset if I start crying," he said.

Carmelita could feel the weakness hitting her like a wave. Her immediate thought was cancer, and she wondered which of these precious people in her life was taking on that battle.

"It's nothing like that," Rick assured her, and he slowly began detailing his dream.

Rick had lived with the dream long enough that he now could tell the details smoothly, and the story poured from him with all of the emotion he had felt from the moment he first woke up. It was not as if the story faded for him; instead, it seemed to snowball, becoming more heart-wrenching for him each time he told it. He talked of having found an adoption agency to assist him in his search, and, finally, he produced his dossier of paperwork and pulled Armando's drawing from it.

Carmelita could feel emotion swelling in her heart as Rick talked, but as she looked into the enormous eyes staring up at her from the drawing, she could not contain her feelings. Tears slipped from her eyes and she physically felt the sadness emanating from the tiny child in the drawing before her. However, despite her feelings of compassion for this child, she could not ignore what this meant to her own family. Her questions were pointed directly at Stephanie.

"What about you?," she asked, genuinely concerned for her daughter-in-law. Through the course of her life, Carmelita had become familiar with the scenario in which the man receives the vision and the woman does the work. Knowing that adding a small child to their family would dramatically increase Stephanie's workload, Carmelita's first concern was how it would affect her first-born's wife.

Stephanie hadn't expected her mother-in-law's response, but her heart held all the answers. She explained that the power of this dream, this vision, was so strong that it was beyond anything they could explain or argue with.

"It's something we have to do," she replied.

"Do you know what you're getting yourself into?" Carmelita asked, not able to shake her pragmatic nature.

Stephanie smiled. "I have no idea."

Her words could not have been more accurate. Stephanie realized that she was in the midst of something too powerful to rationalize, and as she became more familiar with the events unfolding around her she knew that her life was going to change in profound ways. Trying to explain those events, even to herself, was an impossible task and she had accepted the fact that faith alone would lead them on this journey together.

Carmelita's eyes were wet with tears and she felt an overwhelming sense of pride in Rick and Stephanie. It was humbling to see two people so steadfast in their faith that they were able to walk ahead, unable to see the road before them but sure-footed in each step and each other. The lengths that they already had gone to in an attempt to find this child confirmed to Carmelita that they were following a divine directive. Rick and Stephanie had never mentioned adoption, had never alluded to the desire of having more children. But the silent pleas of a helpless child had changed all that, and Carmelita felt love and compassion flooding her own heart.

Beside her, Richard had sat quietly as Rick told his story. The detail and emotion that colored the story told Richard that this was no ordinary dream, no ordinary mission. He immediately accepted, word for word and without a doubt, everything that came from his son's mouth as they sat at their corner table. Something had changed inside of Rick, and his father could see it. Although Rick had been a Christian for most of his life, Richard had never seen him this intent on accomplishing something. Rick was placing his heart in the hands of the Lord, trusting God to lead him to the child he already knew as his daughter.

As Rick turned to his father and asked him what he thought, the elder Silanskas could feel the lump growing in his throat. He cleared his throat, took a deep breath and looked into the tear-dampened eyes of his son.

"I have no doubt that you'll find her," he said. Richard already felt love for this little girl, already knew that she was his granddaughter. It was not something he could explain, it was simply something he knew in his heart.

"I can already see her, son. I already love her. Now go find her."

His father had always been Rick's mentor and guide, and to hear those words coming from Richard meant more than Rick could put into words. Beyond his father's encouragement, however, was the amazement over his mother's acceptance.

It was no secret that Carmelita had reservations about adoption. While she loved children and certainly believed that each and every child deserves to be raised in a loving home, she didn't feel that she would be able to accept as flesh and blood a child that was not actually part of their lineage. That question had first surfaced years earlier, when her middle child, Dianne, had been told that she would not be able to conceive. It was a crushing blow to the family, as Dianne was born to be the kind of nurturer who seems ready-made for motherhood. Knowing that she must have children in her life, Dianne had looked at the possibility of adoption, and Carmelita was vocal in her opinion on the subject.

But to everyone's surprise, that same dismay never crossed Carmelita's mind as Rick told her about the young daughter he and Stephanie were searching for. It wasn't as if Rick and Stephanie had wanted another child, and it was not as if this child appeared to them in a natural way. To family members, her immediate love and acceptance of this child was almost as miraculous as Rick's dream itself. .

Even by her own admission, such feelings took Carmelita by surprise. And both those feelings and her surprise would only escalate in the months that followed.

With his parents now aware of the changes in Rick and Stephanie's life, Rick was eager to tell Dianne and Vince his news. It was a relief to finally share his heart with others, to openly talk about what had, initially, felt like an overwhelming secret. The acceptance he found each time he told the story only solidified his faith and determination, and he knew that Dianne, his cherished younger sister, would share his news with an open heart.

Dianne was no stranger to miracles herself. Despite the doctors' repeated prognosis, Dianne now was the mother of two happy, healthy children. She had, in fact, accepted her fate and was scheduled to undergo a hysterectomy when God intervened. As she was being prepared for surgery, an ultrasound failed to find the tumors that had prompted the scheduled operation, and amazed doctors could find no trace of problems in her body. Just a few months later, she met John Garvis, the man who would become her husband and the father of her children.

It was events such as that which allowed the Silanskas family to talk freely of miracles and to be apologetic when they are surprised by God's handiwork. They had learned, through years of experience, to identify the subtle movements of God and take action, thus opening the door for miracles to walk through. When Rick showed up, unannounced, on Dianne's doorstep, she had no idea that he was about to add to the family's logbook of life-changing events.

It was unusual for him to just appear at her home, and like others in her family before her, Dianne's immediate thoughts jumped to illness. Her husband, John, was at work that Thursday morning, giving the brother and sister time to discuss things one-on-one.

"There's something I have to tell you," he said, and Dianne suddenly noticed the folder of papers he was carrying. Her heart and mind were racing as they walked to her dining room table.

With the same clarity and precise detail with which he had told the story before, Rick again led Dianne through the story of the little girl with the big brown eyes that he had found standing alone in the dilapidated basement. It was a moving story, one that resonated all the way to Dianne's soul. As he showed her the little girl's picture and explained that they already had contacted an adoption agency, Dianne misunderstood the reason for his visit.

"Rick, are you asking John and me to adopt her?"

Rick clutched the pile of papers close to his chest, hugging them as if the little girl was nestled somewhere deep inside of them.

"Oh, no, no, no … you can't have her! She's ours, Dianne. We're going to find her and adopt her."

Those words were even more surprising to Dianne than if he had asked her to adopt the child. His siblings and parents had watched for years as Rick had put the needs of his children before his own. Although Rick's musical career had done well, he had not achieved the kind of success his family felt he was due. Dianne, like others in the Silanskas clan, had naturally assumed that once his children had grown, Rick would finally get the chance to devote himself to his music. She had envisioned that he would be performing concerts on a grand scale, touring the world and sharing his gift of music.

Dianne could tell that Rick's entire focus had changed. His heart was breaking for this child; already, he looked like a parent whose child was missing and he was determined against all odds to find her. Dianne's heart went out to him, knowing that he was being sent on a mission for which he hadn't enlisted, but knew he had to answer the call.

Her heart went out to her older brother, and she looked at the sadness and urgency in his eyes. She had no doubts that he would find this child, but she ached for the pain of his journey. Her eyes fell upon her watch, and she realized she had to rush her brother through this moment.

"I am so sorry, Rick. I feel so bad – but I have to get Sarah to dance practice."

Rick understood, but as Dianne drove her six-year-old to practice, her heart was filled with her brother's sadness. She felt overwhelmed by what she had seen in his eyes. As she signed in her daughter for that day's practice, she found herself tearfully pouring out the story to the woman at the front desk.

She wanted so badly to do something for Rick, to help the big brother who had, unfailingly, been there for her. He had always had a big heart, had always known how to make people feel loved and special, and as a result, everyone wanted to be around him. She was aware of how fortunate she had been to grow up with him, and the closeness they had shared as children had blossomed with time.

And even though Dianne was happy that Rick found his true soul mate in Stephanie, she had cried for three days straight after they married, grieving the loss of her best friend. He had been there on so many days in so many ways, she wanted only to be able to give some of that back.

Dianne's mind drifted back to Sarah's first day of school, and how that first-time separation had left her in a flood of maternal tears. It was Rick she had turned to, Rick who had comforted her by telephone every morning as she lamented the daily loss of her baby. Now, at a time when he felt the same type of loss, she felt inadequate to help. The only thing Dianne knew to do in a situation like this was to pray, but at this moment, she wasn't even sure of what she was praying for.

The annual Toy Show at the Orlando Convention Center had become a family event for the Silanskas brood. In 2003, it fell on January 11, and Rick and his sons, Andrew and Tony, joined Vince and his wife, Cris, to attend the show. Despite the fact that she was seven months pregnant with their second son, Cris happily traipsed through the cavernous exhibits, enjoying the Saturday morning with their three-year-old son. Little Vince, as he was called, reveled in the sights and sounds of the day, but after three hours, the crew felt that they had seen enough.

Rick had been waiting for the right moment to tell Vince and Cris about what was happening in his life, and as they walked across the street to FAO Schwartz, he knew that the time had arrived.

"I have something I want to talk to you guys about," he said, and Andrew and Tony took their young nephew inside, knowing what their father was about to say. The weather was uncharacteristically cold as Cris and Vince sat on a bench outside the famous toy store while Rick told them his story.

It wasn't just the cold weather that caused the hair on Cris' arms to stand up. The couple sat there, incredulous, as Rick walked them through the recent events of his life. Vince wondered how Rick had managed to keep so much inside for so long; Rick was typically an emotional man who readily shared what was on his heart. And Vince, who worked side by side with him at their DreamVision offices, was amazed to hear the dramatic story unfold. Rick told them of his search for the little girl, of knowing in his heart that she was in Russia and of being absolutely determined to find her.

The response was typical of Vince's reaction to his big brother.

"What can we do to help?" he asked, and Rick once again felt gratitude for the openness and concern of his close-knit family.

"Just pray," he told them. "I've got to find her. I know she's out there. Just pray for us."

The questions and concerns were not unlike those that already had been voiced by Rick's mother. As a mother herself, Cris realized that the care taking duties would fall upon Stephanie, who had already raised four children. This was the time in their lives when circumstances were supposed to become easier for the parents, the time when they would finally get the opportunity to enjoy everything they had sacrificed to meet the needs of a growing family.

Rick assured them that Stephanie was behind him, completely, in this plan. He explained that God had prepared her heart, and there was no other explanation for her immediate willingness to join him in the search. Cris' mind then went to her nieces and nephews.

Again, Rick promised her, the kids were fine with it. Cris and Vince felt stunned, as if they were at the center of a surreal experience. It was only as they made the hour-long drive to their home in Clermont that they were able to begin talking about what had just happened.

Adoption was a subject that the couple had already broached in the privacy of their own home. Cris and Vince had married in 1995, and even before Little Vince was born four years later, Cris had talked about feeling led to adopt a little girl. Vince's birth only seemed to reinforce that desire, and Cris felt in her heart that they would probably adopt an Asian child.

But a few months before Rick's dream, Cris and Vince had noticed an older American couple while attending an event at Disneyworld. The couple had two beautiful young girls who caught Vince's eye, and he was so enamored with the children that he couldn't resist complementing the couple on their beautiful, well-behaved daughters. It was then that he learned the girls had been adopted from a Russian orphanage, and the experience sparked a new discussion between Cris and Vince.

Both were still open to adopting a little girl from another country, but now Vince felt strongly that they should consider Russia. As Rick told them his story, both had experienced an eerie combination of feelings. It was as if the very thing they had wanted was happening to Rick, and they found themselves amazed. How could it be that the very thing they had discussed, the very plan they fully intended to carry out one day, was happening in their family – but not to them? Was this a matter of faith, and they weren't ready to take such a monumental leap?

As they sat with the news, digesting and becoming more comfortable with it, they realized this simply was not their time. God knows which doors to open, and they realized that a larger plan was already in place. Now, they knew, was the time for them to help Rick and Stephanie in whatever way they could and, like everyone else around them, wait and see what happened.

The waiting, under Rick and Stephanie's roof, took on different meanings for different family members. Stephanie watched as Jessica and Andrew, the only two children still living at home with them, grew more comfortable with the idea of having a new little sister. While the news had, understandably, hit them from out of the blue, they gradually tried the information on for size, giving it time to sink in and become reality.

For eleven-year-old Andrew, it seemed a tardy answer to a long-time request. As the baby of the family, Andrew had, for years, asked Stephanie why he couldn't have a baby brother or sister. Now, it seemed, his wish was going to come true. Both he and Jessica cautiously introduced the idea to friends at school, only to learn that adoption was not such an unusual concept. Everyone, it seemed, either knew someone who had been adopted or knew of someone who had adopted a child.

It was becoming a reality in every sense of the word. Rick and Stephanie had put in long hours filling out the required paperwork to get their home approved for international adoption, and Rick made frequent trips to the state capitol of Tallahassee to get the official documents in hand. He wasn't about to let the process be slowed by the U.S. Postal Service, and had no qualms about jumping in the car and making the six-hour drive to retrieve a single piece of paper.

But even as the process moved forward, the days seemed torturously slow for Rick. He ached to find that little girl, was filled with questions about who she was and where she came from. There had been no more dreams since that one, life-changing night, but Rick clung steadfastly to those two moments, becoming more certain with each passing day that God would reveal the girl's whereabouts to them soon.

At his office in Thomasville, Georgia, Ed Thomas was fielding phone calls from Rick daily. Nothing about this case had been typical from the beginning, and so he wasn't surprised to see it progressing in unusual ways. Ed felt Rick's growing urgency and did his best to remind Rick that it could take awhile.

"When do you think we'll find her?" Rick asked Ed shortly after he and Stephanie had completed all the paperwork for the home study.

Ed had a strong feeling about this case, a feeling he had never experienced in all his years of working with potential adopters.

"The way this is going," he told Rick, "I think that we'll find her when the time is right. I think once the home study is completed, she'll be revealed to us."

Rick clung to the words like a drowning man to a life raft. He even repeated them to others, saying that he was sure they would find the girl as soon as his home study was done and they had received approval for adoption. Ed knew that such approval could take up to two months, and in his heart he was concerned for Rick. Rick's desire to find her only intensified with each moment that passed, and it seemed incomprehensible that he could continue with this kind of stress and uncertainty for two months.

It was rare for Ed to visit the home of clients, but when the opportunity presented itself, he realized this would be one worth taking. He had reason to be in Orlando for business, and he made plans to visit Rick and Stephanie at their home.

He already had warned the couple that many orphanages were in rural areas without access to technology. Therefore, finding the girl in the drawing could be more complicated than it was in other countries. They had faxed the drawing to Russian officials and orphanages, but matching the girl could take awhile. As Ed visited their home, he was able to give them one piece of hope.

"We have a woman who was a past adoptive mother in Russia, and she sent me something I think you'll be interested in," he said. At Ed's request, Rick led him to the computer, and Ed pulled up a website. He walked Rick through the translation software, explaining that this was something new that an orphanage was trying. It wasn't a public website but was, instead, a database for a baby home in Pechory, near the Estonian border.

Ed pulled the site up on the screen, and Rick found himself touched by what he saw. About one hundred children were listed on the site, and although it was a long shot, Ed felt it would give Rick something to look at. Rick flipped through the pictures, hoping to find his lost little girl. The experience was heartbreaking, not only because he could not find her, but because he was shaken by the seemingly endless sea of lost, lonely eyes that stared back at him from the website. Beside each picture was a date of birth and a first name, and it provided Rick with a gut-wrenching glimpse into a land of aching hearts.

"I don't know where you'll find her," Ed said, "but here's something you might want to keep an eye on."

The site became a regular part of Rick's routine. He pulled it up several times a day, but soon realized that nothing new was being added from one visit to the next. Still, he was strangely compelled to continue visiting it, as if it provided him with some sort of bridge between the world he lived in and the world he wanted so desperately to discover.

Back at school in Orlando, Rick's oldest son, Tony, continued having concerns about his father's recent news. He was accustomed to seeing his dad throw himself wholeheartedly into unorthodox situations, but this was beyond anything that Rick had surprised them with in the past. While he still believed in his father, he also knew he was no longer a child who was blind to his parents' human foibles.

Knowing that he had to address his concerns, he called Rick and asked if they could meet for dinner.

They had dinner at a seafood restaurant near Tony's Orlando campus, and the meal went as they usually did, with easy conversation between father and son. Rick knew that Tony had a reason for calling him there, but also knew that whatever was on his son's mind must come out on his son's terms. Rick didn't push the subject, and as they left the restaurant, Tony paused and said they needed to talk.

Tony shared his father's expressive brown eyes, and as Rick watched, he saw those familiar eyes fill with intensity and sincerity.

"I really believe that something has happened to you, Dad," Tony began, assuring his father that he trusted every word that his father had spoken was true. "I just want to know that you've thought this all through. That you've thought about what it means for Mom…"

It was as if Rick were watching his little boy grow into a man right before his eyes, and he felt as if his heart would burst with pride and gratitude. He could still see Tony as an infant, could still feel that precious little boy in his arms, yet before him he saw a concerned and responsible young man who wanted to protect his family.

A quick prayer of gratitude flashed through Rick's mind before he addressed his son's concerns. As they talked, Rick explained that he had not only thought this through, but that God had put it in his heart to do this task. He explained that he wasn't able to walk away, even if he wanted to, because he knew, as certain as he had known anything in his life, that she was out there waiting for him. And he simply had to answer that calling, because a child's life – <u>his</u> child's life – was at stake.

As Tony listened, his eyes and heart filled with awe and wonder at his father's faith. He was excited for Rick's mission, but beyond that he was overwhelmed by his father's ability to continue on a path that others might not have even seen.

"You know what you remind me of, Dad?"

Rick shook his head and watched his elder son, not sure where this was headed.

"You're like – in the Bible, where the one sheep got away. And the shepherd has to go looking for it. He can't do anything else. That's how I look at you. You're the shepherd who won't let anything happen to that sheep."

Rick's heart was flooded with emotion and his eyes filled with tears. It was an eloquent and touching end to an evening between father and son, and Rick found himself deeply affected by Tony's analogy. As they parted ways and Rick made the ninety-minute drive back to his home in Lady Lake, he found himself lost in his son's words. His soul was stirred by Tony's faith, but Rick also found himself moved by the fact that Tony had such faith in his own faith. All Rick needed now was a miracle at the other end of the world.

Chapter Five

As his family and friends settled into the dawn of the new year, Rick found himself consumed with thoughts of the little girl he firmly believed to be in Russia. The intensity that he had felt after his dream had only grown with time, and the strain of his search already was beginning to show.

Now that those close to him were aware of what he was dealing with, Rick felt a sense of relief that comes from sharing a burden. But at the same time, his anxiety over finding the missing child continued escalating.

Rick was, in the eyes of those closest to him, a man on a mission. And while everyone near him had seen Rick set off on lofty quests before, this was beyond what anyone could have predicted. He became completely preoccupied with the little girl, entirely absorbed with reaching a successful resolution to this mystery.

Work, like everything else, took a back seat to Rick's vision. After telling his parents and siblings about the new journey he and Stephanie had embarked upon, he cautiously began approaching more friends with his news.

It was not the type of news he could blurt out in a phone conversation; each time he related the story, it was a personal and emotional encounter. One that both reinforced his belief in his mission and heightened his sense of urgency.

Joe Lyons had first met Rick in the late nineties, when the two men worked together on a film. Although the movie was largely dismissed by critics, it laid the foundation for a lasting friendship between the two men, and it also put Rick in contention for a possible Academy Award nomination for "Best Musical Score."

He and Joe had stayed in touch in the years that followed, always wanting to work together but never seeming to find the right time. In recent months, they had discussed Rick's inclusion on an upcoming project being considered by Joe's production company, but it seemed that one interruption after another prevented them from getting together to finalize the plan.

Rick felt that Joe would be open to the story of what was happening to the Silanskas family, but he also knew that it had to be presented carefully and accurately. He called Joe, whose production company was housed on the Universal Studios lot.

When he answered his telephone that day, Joe wasn't particularly surprised to hear from Rick. It was Rick's sense of urgency that they meet for lunch that caught him off guard. After months of schedules refusing to cooperate and being able to connect, this time they somehow managed to make a lunch date before hanging up the phone.

From the moment they met at a Denny's Restaurant just down the street from the studios, Joe knew something was happening to – or, more accurately, within – Rick. Joe had long been amazed by Rick's steadfast faith, viewing him as something of a disciple. Rick was so committed in his faith that it seemed to Joe he had a direct pipeline to God. As Rick related his story, he only confirmed Joe's belief.

Joe listened, fascinated, as Rick told the story in painstaking detail. He remembered elements that most people never see in a dream, and Joe felt a supernatural shiver run through his body as he listened. Rick was electrified and urgent, his face filled with a kind of determination that Joe recognized from previous encounters with other parents.

Joe's years as an Orlando police officer had ended in 1991 after a scuffle with a rapist had left his knee permanently injured. During his years on the force Joe had seen it all, and in Joe's mind, Rick's demeanor matched that of a parent who was filing a report on a missing child. Rick was both distraught and determined; emotional and passionate. Joe recognized the sincerity and pain of a grieving parent, and he left the restaurant that day completely convinced that, not only did that little girl exist, but that Rick would find her.

Had it been anyone else, Joe would later admit to himself and to others, he would have dismissed the story as a haunting but fleeting dream. Rick had recounted the dream so vividly, and coupled with the intensity of his determination to find the child, it left Joe without any doubt that what Rick had experienced was nothing short of a miracle in the making.

"Rick, this is going to be a movie someday," he said, not really thinking about the words as they left his mouth. "You've got to start documenting this. You need to start filming some of this, get it on tape, because when it all happens, nobody is going to believe you."

Rick was much too absorbed in his thoughts of the little girl to give any weight to Joe's words. Besides, he explained, he wasn't in the movie business. His company had found success creating television commercials and jingles for clients. Early in December, he and Vince had met over dinner and had outlined DreamVision's strategy for the year ahead. The brothers had inked a blueprint to rebuild the company as a major advertising agency, and that agenda certainly did not include movies.

Besides, to Rick, this had nothing to do with credibility, it was about a little child's life. There was nothing else filling his mind, only thoughts of finding, and bringing home, the little girl from the dream. Whether or not people believed him was something that he was already discovering would have to be dealt with on a case-by-case basis.

The lunch meeting served as more than a springboard for Rick to share his story; it also prompted the two men to rethink their working relationship. They had liked one another from the moment they met and had vowed to some day work side by side, but as Joe left the meeting, something inside of him clicked. He was deeply moved by what Rick had just told him, and he now believed, more than ever, that he wanted to work with Rick, not just occasionally but as part of his daily routine.

For Rick, the meeting served an entirely different purpose. He was relieved to have his story so openly and warmly received by Joe, grateful that his words were accepted as truth. While his family had readily listened to his story and given their support, not everyone was as willing to believe in the events that were unfolding.

Of all those he told, he was most hurt – and shocked - by the reaction from his friend and spiritual brother, David. He had told David about his dream almost immediately after he had informed his family, and he had expected a much different response.

Rick had known David for more than fifteen years, and through the years they had grown both as friends and as spiritual advisers to one another. Rick had a deep respect for David, loving him like a brother and cherishing the friendship as a rare and precious gift. It was only natural, then, that David would be one of the first people Rick called when he felt ready to share his story.

They had met for dinner at a restaurant in Leesburg, and Rick was bursting with the story. He wasn't sure what to expect from others; Rick knew that his story was an unusual one, but of all the people in his life beyond his immediate family, he trusted most that David would hear his words and be ready to support Rick on the journey he was making.

Rick told the story of his dream, of finding The Open Door Adoption Agency, of meeting with Armando and watching as the same child from his dream rose from the artist's tablet. David continued eating while Rick spoke, and it was only when Rick had finished his story that David rested his fork on his plate and met Rick's gaze.

"Rick," he began, as Rick studied his friend's face, not certain of what he was reading in the eyes he thought he knew so well. David cleared his throat and looked away for a fleeting moment, then looked back across the table.

"I have a real hard time believing all of this. And, truly, I question God's presence in all of this."

Rick sat for a moment, stunned and uncertain of what to say. He heard the words slipping out of his mouth before he even had time to think them through.

"But I don't," he replied.

The two men sat across the table from one another and Rick felt a chill between them that had never been present in their relationship before. He had, at the very least, anticipated that David would support him through prayer, would offer some sort of spiritual insight into what was occurring. Instead, he only reiterated his doubt in what Rick was experiencing.

It was as if a chasm had suddenly been carved into the earth between them. Rick looked at this longtime friend, wondering what had happened. As they parted ways that night, Rick knew that this rift would not soon be healed, nor did he know what it was based on.

Driving home in the dark, his heart ached from the sharp edge of David's words. Then, as he recalled the dream where he first saw the little girl, he felt the shiver of realization sweep through his body.

In that dream, he had been standing on the stairs with three men whom, he had no doubt, knew him very well – yet he did not know them. The hot stinging of tears burned his eyes as he realized the significance of what had just occurred with David, realizing that his dream had been accurate. David was not the man he thought he knew.

The experience put a sense of hesitation into each telling of the story; Rick realized that if such a dear, longtime friend could turn his back on him at a time like this, there was nothing to keep others from doing the same. At the same time, he found it impossible not to share the story, and when it was met with the kind of reception it received from Joe, Rick found himself extremely grateful and appreciative for their belief in him. Each time someone accepted his story, Rick could feel the flood of gratitude; at the same time, it served as a painful reminder of David's rejection.

Although winter is known for its short days, each one seemed like an eternity to Rick. Regardless of how much he had to accomplish, each day moved at a torturously slow pace for him; nothing mattered to him except finding that little child, and as the hours would drag on before disappearing into nightfall, he found himself counting every minute. Every moment was spent waiting for the phone to ring, waiting for word on where this tiny little girl was waiting for him. He checked the web site from the Russian orphanage constantly, even though it had not been changed or updated in any way since the first day he saw it. But each visit to that site stirred him more, and it kept Rick acutely aware of the plight facing the many young orphans in Russia.

Their situation, he was learning, was nothing short of tragic. Nearly a million children lived in orphanages, hospitals and baby homes in Russia, and adding to the tragedy were the laws that prevented many of them from being adopted. Unless a parent specifically signed paperwork to terminate all parental rights, their child could not be adopted. Instead, that child would be raised as a ward of the state until they reached the age of seventeen, at which time they would be handed a small sum of money and are left on their own.

Rick was stunned to learn about the dire need of the orphans; in many cases, parents had become so poverty-stricken that they had no choice but to leave them in orphanages. In other cases, the parents would simply abandon the children on the street, hoping they would be found and cared for by strangers. However, if they didn't sign over their rights, the opportunity still existed for them to one day reclaim their child. For the child, it meant that they would not be eligible for adoption to another family.

The more Rick discovered about international adoption procedures, the stronger his urge became to get involved and affect change. He began discussing with Stephanie the idea of creating a non-profit foundation that could offer financial assistance to potential adoptive parents who wanted to give a home to a Russian child. The costs, he now knew, were prohibitive – adoptions from Russia cost between thirty thousand and fifty thousand dollars. As he looked at the young faces on the website, he became more and more driven to help make it easier for those abandoned children to be placed in the loving homes they longed for. Determined to make a lasting improvement in the lives of the children he saw on his computer screen, he began mapping out a plan for a new foundation.

As usual, Stephanie was supportive of his vision and they discussed the potential for change as well as the obstacles they would have to overcome to create such a foundation. She recalled a sermon she had heard about a woman named Anna, based on a Bible passage in the book of Luke.

Anna, she recalled, was a prophetess who was widowed at an early age and spent the rest of her life in the temple, serving God through prayer and fasting. Her years of servitude were rewarded when she was given the prophecy of Jesus' birth, which she used to encourage Mary and Joseph.

The name "Anna" seemed fitting as a moniker for their mission; it represented the kind of unwavering, steadfast faith they needed to perform the tasks that now were foremost in their minds. With The Project Anna Foundation beginning to take shape, Rick turned to his younger brother to help start building a ministry.

From the moment that Rick told Vince about his dream of the little girl, Vince knew that their lives and plans were changing. It quickly became evident that the goals and game plan for DreamVision that they had developed just a few weeks earlier no longer fit. Everything around them was shifting, and none of them had the faintest idea of where the story would end. Each day was a fresh adventure in unchartered territory, with Vince researching the financial aspects of creating a ministry and Rick focusing on the purpose and mission of Project Anna.

Vince had never seen Rick so focused on any one single mission. Each day, it seemed, Rick grew more intense, more sure-footed in the path he was following. Rick now realized that the projects his company took on were not his reason for being here; they were the means to an end, the vehicles that would provide them with the necessary income to build their ministry.

Rick's meeting with Joe Lyons had done more than just solidify a longtime friendship, it also reinforced both men's desire to work together. Joe met with Rick again, this time joined by Vince as well, and they began hammering out the details of Joe's role in the changing DreamVision agenda. Joe would officially come on board as a producer, but his contributions to the company went far beyond that. Since leaving the police force Joe had carved out a solid and well-connected reputation in the film industry, and he had access to individuals and resources that DreamVision would need to reach the next level.

The excitement in the air was electric; each day was an adventure that was taking the company to places that remained a mystery, even to key players. Rick's team was loyal, willing to follow him to the end of the earth, and as he continually re-shaped the DreamVision mission, his small group of workers remained certain that he had seen something they hadn't. They followed him unfailingly, not questioning his actions but rather trusting in his reasons.

Even as he led, Rick continued feeling consumed with a sense of urgency. The child from his dream stayed first and foremost in his mind. With his home study paperwork completed, there was nothing to do but wait and wonder when he would finally discover who – and where – that child was.

As the vision for The Project Anna Foundation took shape, Rick and Vince became more urgent about telling the story behind it and generating business that would allow them to pour more money into helping the Russian orphans.

One of the ideas that had been abandoned during Rick and Vince's December strategy session was the dream of creating wholesome animated children's films. Rick had spent much of the past six years cultivating a team of animators who could provide top-quality 3D animation for films and he dreamed of providing the industry with child-friendly films reminiscent of Disney's earlier days. He had studied Walt Disney's work extensively and as he grew more disgusted with what was happening within the film industry, he had taken it upon himself to develop an animated segment of his business. The idea was to create children's films that returned to the innocence of Disney's work while at the same time generating the kind of eye-popping animation from studios such as Pixar.

The idea, they knew, was a good one, but they had not gelled in terms of what films they would be able to offer. Although they had pushed the idea aside as they set out to generate business for their advertising agency, this new direction inspired them to revisit the idea once again.

Rick and Vince were meeting daily with potential clients and investors, feverishly pursuing new ways of doing business. The mission seemed very clear to them at this point: They would get funding for films and projects that would, upon their success, allow the company to grow The Project Anna Foundation. They began talking about a series of animated children's films and Rick was able to arrange a lunch meeting with Charlie Spell, a producer and potential investor.

They met over lunch at the Cheesecake Factory in Winter Park, and Rick had prepared his pitch to sell Charlie on the animated film series. He had never met the man before, had only talked to him on the phone, but he felt completely comfortable as they sat down together.

Rick began his prepared spiel, but as he talked, something came over him. He halted himself, mid-sentence, and took a deep breath.

"You know," he said, looking across the table at Charlie, "I gotta tell you something. I don't know how you're going to take this, but I have something I just have to share with you."

As he had done so many times with so many people over the past few weeks, Rick again began telling the story of standing on those crumbling basement stairs and seeing the precious, lost little child looking up at him. Each time he told the story it felt as if he were living it again, as if he was so close to holding that little girl in his arms once more. He could feel her in his arms as he talked, and the emotions that were so close to the surface welled up into Rick's eyes.

He reached into his briefcase and pulled out the picture Armando had drawn, explaining that he and his wife had completed all the needed paperwork and, as soon as they found her, they were adopting this very child.

Charlie sat silently, transfixed by Rick's story and touched by his passion. He listened quietly, his fork in mid-air, as Rick finished his tale. The two men sat across from one another in silence for a moment.

"That's your movie," Charlie said.

"What?"

"Your animated children's movie. That's it. You've got to make this story into a movie."

Suddenly, the idea made perfect sense to Rick. His mind began reeling with possibilities and he played scenes out in his head. Of course they could do this as an animated film! What better way to raise awareness among adults while at the same time creating a heart-warming story for children?!

He called Vince as soon as he was back in his car. The excitement spilled through the phone; it was nothing short of electric. They immediately set out to create a plot and then began scheduling meetings with those who could bring it to fruition.

Despite all of the excitement and energy being generated within the business, Rick continued wrestling with patience. He called Ed Thomas daily, wanting to know if they had heard anything yet. Each time, Ed was patiently reassuring, telling him that they didn't know anything new but confirming that he felt each day brought them just a little bit closer in their search.

Rick would call up the web site, hoping to one day see something changed on the site; see new photos added, see the face of a child matching the drawing that also was burned into his mind. But each visit to the site just brought the same photos he had seen the day before, brought him no new faces to look at.

Rick and Vince began seeking out meetings to pitch the idea of their animated film, and it gave Rick the opportunity to share, time and time again, the story of his dream and the little child in the basement. With each meeting, he brought along her picture, using it to explain that he was in the process of finding her. It didn't matter if they believed him or not; Rick knew in his heart he was following God's intended path for him, and he wasn't about to miss an opportunity by remaining silent. He was infused with an energy and passion that could not be explained, nor could it be matched; Rick had never been so certain of anything in his life, and he knew he would find this child. He just didn't know when.

The waiting game that he and Stephanie had to play didn't come with a set time frame. Ed Thomas had cautioned them that it takes up to sixty days for the paperwork to be processed. Rick knew they potentially had a long wait, and he prayed each day that God would expedite the process, allowing them to find that little girl quickly.

The meeting he and Vince had scheduled for the morning of January 18 had been cancelled, so Rick again found himself at his desk, staring at the web site from the Russian orphanage. He wasn't sure that they ever updated it, but he still found something oddly comforting just by visiting it. As he checked it again that morning, he saw nothing was new; the site still listed twelve pages of orphans, twelve pages of faces that Rick had become so familiar with during the past three weeks.

He closed his laptop and turned his attention to some paperwork and was relieved when the phone rang. His secretary, Jennifer, buzzed the phone in his office.

"Hey, Rick, Stephanie's on line one," she said.

Rick picked up the phone.

"Hi there!" he said, always happy to hear from his wife.

"I just wanted to let you know – we just got that fax from the adoption agency. That should be everything they need."

Rick breathed a heavy sigh of relief.

"Oh, Steph! That's wonderful!"

Rick felt the burden he had carried in his heart lightening. They had been waiting on that one, final piece of paperwork, and Rick knew that until they received it, they could not be approved for adoption. Even if they found the child, they would not be able to adopt her until the paperwork was finalized. Now, he believed, their search could begin in earnest.

Rick was happy and upbeat as he hung up the phone. Less than a month had passed since he had first met this little girl in that decrepit basement, yet he felt like this had dragged on for years.

Rick opened his laptop, knowing it was fruitless to check the web site again, but unable to resist.

Rick navigated the now-familiar path and watched as the page loaded on his computer. It was the same as always; the same twelve pages of orphans he now felt he would recognize on sight if he ever saw them in person.

"Might as well go to lunch," he thought to himself. He placed his hand on computer mouse and was moving the cursor to close the page when it suddenly reloaded. Rick did a double-take.

Right before his eyes, the information on the site was updated. One new child had been added to the site, it told him. Rick gave a deep sigh. His heart told him what was about to happen. With a trembling hand, he clicked on the new page.

Chapter Six

Nothing in Rick's life could have predicted the chain of events that began unfolding in late December 2002, but every moment he had lived before then prepared him for it.

He entered the world in the usual way on an otherwise nondescript day in June of 1958. Richard and Carmelita lived in Baltimore, where Richard was a salesman and Carmelita was a beautician and housewife. They reveled in the joy of their first child's birth, and from the time their family began, the couple's thoughts were consumed with providing their children all the happiness that life could afford. Both of them worked hard to create a life that, while far from extravagant, was equipped with all the comforts that a childhood should include.

When Richard fell ill with tuberculosis just three months after his son's birth, Carmelita was determined not to let the separation come between father and son. At that time, such an illness demanded that Richard remained quarantined. Carmelita would visit the hospital daily, standing outside Richard's window holding Rick so that father and son could see one another. The hospitalization lasted for an entire year, and during those twelve months, a deep and lasting bond developed between Rick and Carmelita.

With the exception of Richard's hospitalization, he was there for his family in ways that, even as a child, Rick knew was unusual. Later in life, when the demands of Rick's own career kept him away at night, he would marvel at how deftly his father had managed to juggle numerous jobs to keep his family fed, clothed and sheltered, yet at the same time always seemed to be there for them. Regardless of whether it was a music recital or a school play, Rick always knew that he would see both of his parents in the audience. Both Richard and Carmelita were actively involved in the lives of their children, and that involvement never waned, even as the children grew into adults. Placing their children above their own wants and needs, they set an example of giving and sacrifice that remained implanted in Rick's heart and soul for the rest of his life.

Although the family didn't have great stores of wealth, they impressed upon Rick from the beginning that treasures, even the smallest ones, were meant to be shared. Rick learned some of his greatest lessons about giving from watching his mother. Carmelita's actions were based on unconditional love and a strong sense of concern for the world around her. If others were hungry, Rick learned, you fed them. If they were naked, you clothed them. He regularly saw some of the Bible's most basic principles played out in simple but effective ways. Among the most important of these lessons was learning that caring for others was never to be done with strings attached or with fanfare. It was important to give just because there was need, and it should never be done at the sacrifice of the other person's pride or respect.

Giving, he learned, should not come from one's own excess but rather from the needs of others. You didn't give your toys to someone because you had too many, he learned; you gave someone else a toy because they had none. And, more importantly, you did not give what you wouldn't want to receive.

"You don't give someone broken toys," she explained to him. "Would you want to get a broken toy? You only give what you would want to get."

Rick's baby sister, Dianne, was born two years after him, and Vince completed the family three years after Dianne. Shortly after Dianne's birth, the family moved to Catonsville, a white-collar community outside of Baltimore. It was there, inside a large and beautiful house that Carmelita transformed into a home, that the Silanskas family would cultivate some of their richest memories.

Christmas was a particularly magical time for the family, with both Richard and Carmelita often going overboard on decorating, creating an ever-evolving winter wonderland for their children. The scene was ripped from the pages of a Norman Rockwell calendar, with Carmelita cooking incessantly as the holidays neared and Richard filling every bit of space with decorations. The family celebrations would last all the way through New Year's Day, and it seemed that every moment of the holidays was celebrated to the fullest.

Richard created a spectacular Christmas fantasyland with lights and every imaginable combination of Santa and traditional religious decorations. Rick learned early on just how astonishing the sights, sounds and smells of the holidays could be.

One of Carmelita's holiday traditions was to provide her children with new robes, pajamas and slippers each Christmas. Then, on Christmas morning, wearing their brand-new holiday sleepwear, the Silanskas children would run downstairs, almost breathless with excitement, and see the cache of presents that Santa had somehow single-handedly hauled in on his sleigh. Ever the doting dad, Richard made home movies of their Christmas morning discoveries, providing lasting documentation of their visits from the jolly old elf.

It is widely known that Santa never arrives at a home while children are still wide awake. It is fruitless for children to try and keep their eyes open, waiting to hear the sound of reindeer hooves touching down on the roof or hoping to catch a glimpse of Santa as he arrives, somehow soot-free, through the chimney. In the Silanskas' case, however, Santa was willing to make an exception.

Christmas Eve is quite possibly the longest night of the year for every child, and one year as Rick struggled to go to sleep, a commotion downstairs caught his attention. He heard a noise out on the yard, followed shortly by the doorbell. He could hear sleigh bells ringing and muffled voices talking excitedly. Moments later, Carmelita appeared at his bedroom door.

"Come downstairs," she said, helping her children into their new Christmas robes and slippers. "There's someone here to see you!"

Walking down the stairs with his mother, brother and sister, Rick was amazed to discover, sitting in their living room, none other than Santa Claus himself! Rick had no idea how his parents had managed to convince the legendary Saint Nick to make an early stop at their house, but from that moment on he believed in the magic of Christmas with all his heart.

The gifts that awaited Rick under the tree each Christmas could never compare to the less tangible presents his parents passed along. Richard had a tremendous passion for music, and one of the gifts he passed on to Rick at an early age was an appreciation for every form of instrumentation imaginable.

Richard was an accomplished musician in his own right. By day, Richard sold Hammond organs and at night he would play the piano in some of the city's nicer restaurants. Rick idolized his father and was amazed by his command of the keyboard. Richard became one of the area's first musicians to play both the organ and piano simultaneously. Music became an integral part of the family, and they grew up listening to Richard pound out the music of the 1940s and '50s, while at the same time listening to the contemporary music of the time.

By the age of five, Rick was fully consumed with an unquenchable thirst for music. Rick had his own drum set and he would accompany Richard in countless living-room concerts. At the same time, Rick was drawn to the piano and guitar.

His formal training on the piano began at the age of seven under the tutelage of Sister Innocenta, an aging, humorless nun at St. Joseph's Monastery School Convent. She was a strict and thorough teacher, and Rick often noted to himself that the woman never smiled. Still, she knew music well and was more than capable at sharing her knowledge with students.

While Rick loved playing the piano, he wasn't known for studying some of the finer technical aspects of music that Sister Innocenta insisted he learn. Rick wanted only to play, and the paperwork she assigned seemed to be little more than a nuisance in his mind. Since he often failed to prepare himself for the scholastic side of his lessons, he frequently found himself standing outside her door, terrified to ring the bell and reveal his lack of preparation.

Eventually he would summon the courage to press the button and pay his penance for being ill-prepared. The occasional ruler across the back of the hand seemed a small price to pay for simply being able to play and avoiding that distracting paperwork.

Music recitals are usually the payoff for piano students' hard work. Rick's first recital approached, he diligently practiced the two songs that Sister Innocenta had assigned him to play. One was an Indian-flavored piece; the second was more of the classical variety. He spent endless hours in the family playroom, rehearsing the songs for his first live performance. As Rick practiced one evening, a couple of weeks before the recital, Richard entered the room and listened to him play. He nodded his approval, thrilled to see his son developing into such a fine musician at such an early age.

"Hey Rick," he suggested. "Do you want to give your teacher a nice surprise?"

Rick nodded, eager to take advice from a seasoned professional such as his father. Richard sat with his son and began coaching him on a surprise that all of them would remember for the rest of their lives.

The night of the recital seemed to take forever to arrive, and Rick knew, even before it started, that this was only the first of many performances for him. Wearing his standard-issue blue pants, tie and blazer with a white shirt, he already looked the part of a young concert pianist. Richard understood his son's anticipation, and he imparted a piece of advice that night that would remain with Rick for the rest of his life.

"Music doesn't come from your head, Rick, it comes from your heart," Richard told the seven-year-old. "You can play all the right notes and they'll mean nothing. But if it comes from your heart, they'll never forget it."

It seemed like hours before his name was called, and Rick proudly strode to the piano on the stage. His feet barely touched the floor, and it seemed as though his fingers barely touched the keys as he flew flawlessly through his two assigned songs. He played from his heart, just as his father had told him to do, and the music seemed to flow from his fingertips as if by magic.

As Rick completed his task, the audience broke into a polite round of applause. Rather than standing and excusing himself from the piano as Sister Innocenta had instructed him to do, Rick turned to look over his shoulder at the unsuspecting audience.

As he turned, his eyes caught a glimpse of Sister Innocenta, who stood in the wings, watching her students with that familiar, stern glare. Her arms were crossed and it was obvious that she was completely baffled by Rick's actions. Rick's eyes found his parents, who were sitting in the sea of parents, beaming over their son's musical prowess.

"And now, I would like to play a special song that I have prepared as a surprise," Rick said, just as he and Richard had rehearsed. His parents continued smiling while the rest of the audience looked both startled and bewildered. Rick turned to face the piano once again and, as he turned, the look on Sister Innocenta's face told him that he had better play as if his life depended upon it.

The boogie-woogie number that Richard had taught Rick was a far cry from anything else the parents heard that night at St. Joseph's Monastery School Convent. Rick played passionately and from the heart, pounding out a rollicking, uplifting number that drew thunderous applause from the shocked audience. Rick was hooked. He knew this was what he was born to do. As he stood to bow to the appreciative, clapping crowd, he gave a hesitant glance in the direction of Sister Innocenta. On that stern, unyielding face he saw, amazingly – for both the first and last time in his life – the slightest trace of a smile on her lips.

Rick was drinking punch and eating a cookie, basking in the success of his performance, when Sister Innocenta approached him after the recital. The shadow of a smile Rick saw had now been replaced by Sister Innocenta's familiar stern mask. Rick felt his nervousness return as she neared.

"Mr. Silanskas," she began, and he looked up at the older woman, wide-eyed and unsure of what to expect. "That was very good."

Rick heaved a huge sigh of relief, relaxing.

"But don't ever do it again."

Rick knew he would not attempt such an unannounced performance again, at least not on Sister Innocenta's watch, but he also felt a change in the woman who drilled him endlessly on his musical scales. She now knew that she had a true music student, a child who wanted to learn more than the intricacies of the notes. He wanted to learn the music, the heart and soul of the sound, and the experience deepened the weekly lessons for both of them.

Rick had felt the passion of his own performance, and he now knew how powerful it felt to pour his heart out musically. His musical appetite already was voracious, and Richard only fed that craving with a steady diet of fresh sounds. Although Richard's greatest passion was the music he had grown up with in the forties and fifties, his range went far beyond the big-band and boogie-woogie sounds. The family record player held everything from Glenn Miller to Swan Lake to underground acts of the 1960s, such as the English rock madrigal group, Steeleye Span. Nothing was too off-limits to at least listen to, and that musical accessibility allowed Rick to open his mind to an impossibly broad array of sounds.

As he listened, he learned. Rick would stay glued to WCAO radio out of Baltimore and he became a big fan of the Beatles. By the time he was in fifth grade, he had formed his first band, The Atoms.

The band initially came from necessity; as the school talent show approached, Rick was in need of an act. Dianne had a beautiful voice and immediately was tagged as the singer; Rick played piano and found a classmate who played drums. Rather than play the simple songs generally associated with the fifth grade set, The Atoms found its repertoire in the rock songs of the day.

They were unlike the other acts that graced the stage at St. Joseph's, and while they likely weren't going to give the original artists a run for the money, The Atoms became a showpiece of the Catholic school's talent pool. They held practice sessions at the

Silanskas home and became so popular that the sisters of St. Joseph's would take them to a nursing home for aging nuns, where The Atoms would bring a smile to their audience with an ambitious selection of music. What they lacked in musical expertise they more than made up for with enthusiasm, and Rick again saw that playing with his heart allowed him to convey the notes far more easily than if he relied on fingers and talent alone.

Music had become the driving force in Rick's life, but he also was falling in love with film and television. He was twelve years old when it was announced that Baltimore was getting a new television station, WBFF-TV. The UHF station was the first in Baltimore and among the first in the country, and Rick's excitement over the station's arrival could not be contained. He would rise early in the morning before his parents or siblings, dress for school and turn on the television, waiting for the station to appear. After school, he hurried home and turned on the set, seeing if the new station had arrived. Rick spent hours staring at the station's test pattern, each day hoping to be there when the test pattern disappeared and the new television station arrived.

He was there the moment that transition occurred, and Rick was ecstatic as he watched a new television format enter his home. The first program he saw was "Captain Chesapeake," a children's after-school program that featured a live cast of characters entertaining viewers between cartoons. Rick was completely enthralled with what he saw; television captivated him in a way that was similar to music, but somehow different. Whereas music spoke to his heart, television enchanted his mind, and he found himself glued to the medium.

As Rick's interest in television blossomed, so did a passion for films. His maternal grandmother's close association to the business only enhanced his fascination with movies.

Maryland was the only state with a censorship committee, and Carmelita's mother was Mary Avara, one of the board's most outspoken – and subsequently best-known – members. Gov. J. Millard Tawes appointed her the board's chairwoman in 1960, and for the next two decades – until the board was abolished in 1981 – Mary viewed movies five days a week. Every movie that was going to be screened in the state had to be viewed by the censors. Mary was always there, her current knitting project in tow, making certain that the films slipping into the state's theaters were safe for viewing. The board had the power to edit out unsuitable scenes or reject the movie entirely, making Rick's grandmother one of Maryland's most powerful women in the entertainment business at the time.

Her quick wit and outspoken ways made her a celebrity. Mary was never without a quotable saying, and as a result she appeared on such programs as "The Tonight Show with Johnny Carson," "The Mike Douglas Show," "The Merv Griffin Show" and "The Dick Cavett Show." The entire family would escort her on such outings, and backstage Rick and Vince met celebrities such as Soupy Sales and Bobby Darin, not to mention filling their home movie collection with hours worth of memorable reels.

Despite Mary's celebrity status, and colorful though she was, to Rick she was just his grandmother. He relished the opportunity to accompany her to work. There, during countless hours spent in the projection booth, Rick received an education that no school could have provided him. He learned about editing and saw how films were created, then took that newfound information home with him and began applying it to projects of his own.

Using Richard's 8mm movie camera, Rick began filming home movies. They weren't the average slices-of-life that most amateur movies yielded. Instead, Rick's movies had plots and incorporated music, offering a glimpse of what lay in store for his career. His biggest "hit" was, quite literally, his trashiest effort. Using props such as a trash can, a trash can lid and other assorted items common to the suburban yard, Rick and Richard set up the movie camera on a tripod and patiently shot one frame after another, barely moving the objects between shots. When their film project was completed, the home movie showed the items dancing in the driveway, complete with a soundtrack.

In the woods behind their home, he and Vince embarked on countless adventures that took them to worlds far beyond their Maryland address. In the winter, the graceful slopes near their home made the ideal tracks for toboggan runs, and they grew up as children should; playing to their hearts' content in a world that knew no fear or lack.

Rick's greatest challenge as a child came from a physical ailment that was both unusual and somewhat mysterious. Even as a small child, Rick was plagued with nosebleeds that were so severe that he had to be rushed to the hospital on more than one occasion. Doctors blamed faulty sinuses, but could offer few cures to the problem. They repeatedly cauterized the inside of his nose to halt the bleeding, but Richard and Carmelita were warned that the fix was temporary – eventually, they would hit a point where Rick's nose could no longer be cauterized. It brought out Carmelita's overprotective instincts, as just the slightest touch to Rick's nose could prompt a hemorrhage. It was fortunate that Rick's interests gravitated toward music and television, which kept him out of harm's way much more than rough-and-tumble boyish activities would have allowed.

With his parents' encouragement, Rick continued nurturing his creativity. As Christian folk music became popular, Rick began playing the guitar at church, exploring a new kind of music that was taking root all across the United States.

It was an exciting time for music, and it added a new element to the faith that already had played such a strong role in Rick's childhood. His parents both were devout Catholics, with Rick and Vince filling the traditional roles of altar boys, growing up in the church. The Silanskas children attended Catholic school and it seemed the entire family was in church whenever the doors opened. However, the family put its focus more on faith than on theology; Richard and Carmelita emphasized the teachings of the Bible and lived their faith as much as they spoke it.

Richard truly believed that nothing was impossible; he taught his children that if they wanted something, and that desire was based on faith, it would happen.

The family was content with their life in Catonsville, so Richard's news that they were going to move caused disappointment for everyone. Richard, now in electronics sales, had a job opportunity in Delaware. The family found it difficult to leave the home that was so filled with memories, but clung to the knowledge that they had the one thing that made those memories so valuable – they had each other.

The new Sherwood Forest development was still being built when the family moved to Newark, Delaware. The children would accompany Richard to the site, where production had stalled for the winter. To Rick and his siblings, it seemed impossible that they would one day be living in the same space where they now were skating on ice that stood in the home's foundation. As winter gave way to spring, the house finally was completed and the family settled in, making new memories under a new roof. In many ways, they would always miss the home they left behind in Catonsville. Later, when Rick was an adult with children of his own, he would return to that childhood touchstone and walk the grounds, showing his own offspring some of the places where he'd spent his happiest childhood days. But with a new life beginning in Delaware, the Silanskas family moved forward to see what adventures lay ahead of them.

Rick's affinity for the arts continued evolving, as his interests broadened to include musical theater and writing. He was an average student with a passion for English, music and theater classes, but had little use for basics such as math and science. His obsession with music drove his life, and he was thrilled when he learned that St. Mark's High School, where both he and Dianne were students, would be presenting the musical, "The Fiddler on the Roof." St. Mark's was noted for its strong musical productions, and Rick wanted badly to be a vital part of the production.

He auditioned for one of the lead roles and was somewhat disappointed to only snag the role of the Rabbi. Dianne landed a small role in the musical as well. Rick's big moment in the production – when the Rabbi performs the handkerchief dance at the wedding of the Fiddler's daughter – was as vital to him as if he had landed the lead role of Tevye himself.

Rick danced and sang his heart out that night, and the applause that followed reminded him of his moments on the stage for his piano recitals and garage band performances. The stage was becoming home to him, and he wanted desperately to begin making a career of it as soon as possible.

It didn't matter which door gave him entry to the world of entertainment, it only mattered that he found one. The door opened when he was sixteen and landed a job at a small Elkton, Maryland radio station. He worked part-time, duplicating tapes for the station, learning everything he could about the radio business. Just learning it wasn't enough; Rick wanted a shot at putting his new-found knowledge to work.

When the Sunday morning slot came open, Rick jumped at the chance to have a program of his own. It wasn't the time slot that would excite many people; he was on the air from the time the station signed on at 6 a.m. until 1 p.m., and the broadcast was a combination of public service and religious programming. Rick threw himself into the job and discovered that he had the opportunity to incorporate music into the broadcast. The experience broadened his musical vision even farther, introducing him to the new Christian artists that were finding their way onto the radio.

The broadcast experience didn't slake his thirst for the entertainment business, it merely fed his immediate hunger and created an even greater desire within Rick. This was, he knew, what he was born to do. It didn't matter which form it took – music, television, film or radio – he knew it was what he wanted to do with his life. He approached Frank Baker, the general manager of Rollins Cablevision, a station that offered plenty of local programming. Rick knew it would be an excellent place to dip his toe into the waters of television, and he was convinced that he had the right idea for them.

The idea he presented to Frank was for an afternoon kids' show called "The Fun Club." Rick wanted to do a weekly show that would include music and guests. Rick was so passionate about the idea that he was sure Frank would want to include it on his schedule. Frank listened to the sixteen-year-old pitch his television show, and he saw a fire burning within Rick that he knew was too valuable to extinguish.

Frank regretfully explained to Rick that there was no room on the schedule for the show, but he gave Rick the chance to work in the television studio and become entrenched in the environment. It was not a glory job by any means; Rick would arrive at the studio around 6 a.m. and start the coffee, empty the trash cans and clean the floors before heading off to school an hour later. His hard work, unglamorous as it may have been, paid off: When the schedule opened up a few months later, Frank informed Rick that he had permission to launch "The Fun Club" on the air.

Rick reveled in his new job and he dreamed of ways to make the show bigger each week. His biggest competition was himself, and he constantly looked for ways to attract attention to the program.

A huge fan of Elvis Presley, Rick realized that the way to make his mark could lie in the hands of The King. Or at least a reasonable facsimile.

The most popular Elvis impersonator in the area was an artist known by the name of Little El, and Rick knew that wherever he played, fans followed. Rick booked him to perform on "The Fun Club," then began promoting the appearance in such a way that he was able to get his message out but still maintain an air of suspense.

Rather than saying outright who would be on his show, Rick spent a couple of weeks mysteriously alluding to the live television appearance of a very special guest. His careful wording made it sound as if Elvis himself might be appearing on the show, and Rick's excitement built as the show neared. He had no idea of what to expect; the same could be said for the television station.

As "The Fun Club" went on the air, and Little El took the stage with his band, Rick's studio show suddenly had a live audience. It was not a live studio show, but it turned into one on that particular afternoon. Cars filled the parking lot. Elvis fans crammed into the building. Pandemonium at the station created a chaotic scene that took hours to sort out. Rick had never seen so many bodies shoving into such a small space, and as the mayhem broke loose, Frank Baker found Rick in the studio.

"What is going on?!" he asked, baffled by the hordes of screaming fans. "What have you done?"

Rick was on top of the world, thinking, "I have a hit show!" With hundreds of people pushing and shoving their way into his studio, he knew he had found a career, or, perhaps more accurately, his career had found him.

While he continued working on "The Fun Club," Rick had no idea that his life was about to change dramatically. And, as it so often happens, that life-altering decision came from a very simple invitation.

Holy Angels Catholic Church, the church that the Silanskas family now called home, was not your usual, traditional Catholic church. The church had begun something entirely new, something that was growing out of the charismatic Christian movement of the 1970s. When Richard and Carmelita heard about the prayer meetings being offered in the church basement every week, they decided the entire family should at least go see what it was all about.

Rick would never forget his first time of walking into that basement and seeing the circle of people sitting there. The casual, comfortable setting seemed so far removed from the traditional Catholic service. He could actually feel the warmth of the people gathered there, and he knew that what he was experiencing was love in its purest, most genuine form.

Everything about that night left him in awe. They sang new songs, songs of praise and worship that Rick had never heard before. For the first time in his life, Rick heard people giving testimony as to how God was working in their lives. It was something that was unheard of in the traditional church setting, and Rick marveled at the stories he heard.

The group was led by a lay minister named John Penn, and Rick was enthralled by John's very presence. His powerful presence led Rick to believe that John was a direct conduit to the Holy Spirit, and when John prayed it seemed that the presence of the Lord filled the room.

The prayers Rick heard that night were unlike any he had heard before. Unlike the traditional prayers of the church, these conversations with God talked in specifics at a personal level Rick had never known before. It moved Rick in a way he couldn't explain and now it seemed as if he was meeting God in a completely different way.

Until then, Rick had known plenty about God, but as he listened to the prayers of those around him, he felt as if he was so far removed from God. It was the difference between an acquaintance and a friend. Rick wanted to know more about the unconditional love that had become more real to him in the span of just a few minutes.

The family continued going back to the weekly prayer meetings, and at home they discussed new topics with a different sense of spirituality. Their entire family was beginning to change in ways that they all felt but could not yet completely identify.

Each week, John would extend an invitation to those attending the prayer meeting, asking if there was anyone in the room who wanted to relinquish their life to Christ. It didn't take many weeks before Rick was among those who stood in response to John's invitation. He looked over and saw that Vince also was on his feet. Dianne, who had given her life to Christ at the previous week's meeting, went along with Vince for support.

With their parents waiting for them downstairs, the Silanskas siblings joined the small group of people upstairs who accepted John's invitation that night. The small group listened as John shared more about the scriptures and told them what it meant to accept Christ in their lives. Then he began praying with each person individually.

John owned a powerful, commanding voice, and when he prayed the sinner's prayer with Rick, his voice resonated through Rick's ears. There was a presence in the room, a powerful presence of something not of this world, and Rick could feel it wrapping around him as John prayed with him. As Rick accepted Christ into his heart, he felt that he had just made a friend of an acquaintance he had known for years.

John moved on to pray with the others in the room, and Rick stood by a corner window, quietly contemplating everything that was happening at that moment.

John called Vince over.

"Do you want to ask Jesus into your heart?" he asked, and Vince nodded. John prayed with Vince, then laid his hands on Vince's head. Immediately, he threw his hands back as if he'd touched hot coals.

"Boy, are you sick?" he exclaimed, his voice echoing through the otherwise silent room. Vince was frightened by John's visceral reaction and his impassioned voice.

"No sir, I'm fine," Vince replied.

"Are you SURE?" John persisted.

Vince nodded his head, indicating that he felt fine. John put his hands back on Vince's head and they heard Rick say, "I think it's me."

Rick had been standing near the window with his face in his hands, watching the scene with a sense of reverent curiosity. He wondered what kind of "healing" John was alluding to. As he went back to his own thoughts and prayers, Rick felt his face growing damp, but it wasn't the flow of tears. He pulled his hands away from his face and saw they were covered in blood.

Rick looked down and saw that the yellow fabric jacket he was wearing now was completely stained in red, soaked by the blood from his hemorrhaging nose. Horrified, he returned his hands to his face, feeling the blood gush from his nose and slip through his fingers.

John turned to face Rick and immediately told him to raise his hands in the air. Rick did as he was told.

"Now, I want you to thank Jesus for your healing. Right this instant," he said.

Rick did as he was told, thanking Jesus for the healing that had taken place in his life. As he did so, the flow of blood stopped instantly, as if someone had turned off a faucet.

The room was filled with a dramatic pause. Rick stood there, awash in emotions and covered in blood, his jacket soaked through and his face smeared in red. John prayed with him, then took him to the bathroom to clean him up before the entire group returned downstairs to share their story with the rest of those at the prayer meeting.

That night's events would continue changing the Silanskas family for years to come. After the hemorrhage that ended abruptly, Carmelita took Rick to their family doctor to have his nose examined. She said nothing of what had happened in the church that night and didn't tell the doctor why she wanted Rick examined.

The doctor looked into Rick's nose and a puzzled look crossed his face.

"Uh, there...there's nothing wrong here," he said, obviously baffled by what he was seeing.

"What about the cauterizing? How does that look?" Carmelita asked, well aware of the amount of scar tissue that had been created by the repeated treatments of her son's nose.

The doctor looked again.

"There...there's no sign of cauterizing here! These look like brand new nasal passages. What happened here?"

Overjoyed and relieved, Carmelita explained to the doctor what had taken place. For both Rick and Carmelita, it was miraculous confirmation of what had happened in the church that night, and just two weeks later they would receive further confirmation along the New Jersey turnpike.

The family had taken a day trip and stopped at a gift shop along the turnpike. The family used the bathrooms, stretched their legs and browsed the selection of souvenirs carried by the tiny store. Vince wandered over to a display of postcards, and soon began yelling in excitement.

"You guys! Come here! You have to see this – you're not going to believe this!" he exclaimed with such enthusiasm that both his parents rushed to see what the fuss was about.

Vince had pulled a postcard from the rack and was waving it excitedly.

"Look at this!" he said, handing it to them.

The postcard that had caught Vince's attention was a three-dimensional card, and he had never seen such an amazing sight before. Richard and Carmelita exchanged a hopeful look, and then began pulling other 3D cards from the rack to see Vince's reaction. Each one was met with an exclamation of fascination and disbelief. It was then that John's statement about Vince's "healing" made sense.

Vince had been born with a lazy eye, and while doctors were able to correct the direction of his eye, they were unable to do anything about his lack of depth perception. At the roadside gift shop, for the first time in his twelve years on the planet, Vince finally saw the world in the layers in which it existed.

A trip to the optometrist shortly afterwards confirmed that Vince's medical condition had completely disappeared. He would grow up to have perfect vision, and Rick would never have another drop of blood fall from his nose. To the Silanskas family, they were small acts from a very big God, exclamation points that showed how much He cared for them. Nothing was too big – or too small – for the God they now knew, and it lit a fire within the family that could never be extinguished.

Chapter Seven

The renewed faith and enthusiasm within the Silanskas family forever changed Rick's priorities. Although the family had always walked in faith, all of the family members began taking a more intimate approach to their spiritual path. Rick now placed God at the top of his priorities, seeking His wisdom in each and every decision he made.

He graduated from high school a short time after his healing, and Rick desired nothing more than to find a way to use his talents to serve the Lord. He had known for years that he wanted to pursue a career in entertainment. His recent experiences with television and radio led him to pursue broadcast media. Rick chose nearby University of Delaware as the place to polish his talents and learn new skills, but getting a degree was the farthest thing from his mind.

Just as he had viewed the technical side of his childhood piano lessons as nuisances, Rick saw many of the university's required courses as irrelevant. He filled his schedule with the classes he knew would be most valuable to his career, studying the subjects of communications, public speaking and writing.

He had a vision of creating a television station devoted entirely to Christian programming. Rick dreamed of television shows that would have people praying in the studio and would reach viewers with a message of peace and salvation.

At the time, Christian television programming was in its infancy and cable television was just beginning to come into its own. Richard listened to his son's idea and was, at first, unsure of its business potential. As Rick talked, Richard recognized that what

Rick proposed would fill a void in New Castle County that no one else was reaching. He agreed to join Rick on the venture, and they approached the local cable station. They contracted airtime with the station and created a plan to bring Christian programming to the Delaware cable station five nights a week. All they lacked was a studio and equipment.

They found the studio's location in an empty space above the Newark Revival Tabernacle. The pastor, Arthur Hardt, was a kind and helpful man who was open to the new ministry Rick and Richard wanted to bring to the area. He allowed them to build the studio above the church. Rick and Richard then leased the necessary equipment and on October 8, 1976, they went on the air.

Richard's business experience and Rick's broadcast knowledge proved to be a formidable mix. Jesus Is Lord Television Network began as a small nightly venture and grew into one of the region's most innovative stations. Within a year, the network had become extremely popular, although financially it still struggled. The station became a round-the-clock source for Christian programming, providing contemporary Christian programs such as "The 700 Club," "PTL" and "Oral Roberts," but also aired Christian themed movies and children's programs. Richard began hosting a nightly worship program that was sort of a local version of the 700 Club, and in the process became something of a local celebrity.

When they first launched the network, Rick and Richard also created Sonshine Teleproductions, a production company designed to supplement the TV station's income by providing broadcast services. They provided commercials for a variety of clients and their work stretched beyond their immediate area, including some work in Philadelphia. Rick's work had caught the attention of other cable stations, and about a year after they had first launched the cable network, Rick received a phone call that would, once again, take his life in a new direction.

A fledgling cable network named ESPN was going to provide live coverage of a boxing match in Atlantic City, and Rick's name and phone number landed in the hands of the executive assembling the production crew. He explained to Rick that he needed a truck and a crew to produce the live event, and asked Rick if he would be able to accept the assignment. Rick asked if he could call the man back. Rick immediately dialed Richard's number.

"Dad," he said, "you're not going to believe this!"

As he explained what the man needed, he offered a way for them to meet the man's needs.

"What if we go out and get a truck, and just put all our equipment from the studio in it? We can do the show live, and then use it to do our shows, too."

It was unorthodox, but then, so were most of the things they had tried in the television business, and everything was working beautifully. They had nothing to lose.

While Richard went out to lease a truck, Rick returned his previous phone call and accepted the assignment. They called friends, including Rick's best friend and partner, Kim Shelly, who met them at the studio and helped reconfigure the equipment into the truck. In just two days, they built a truck equipped for live television broadcasts, and two days after that, Rick was on the road headed for Atlantic City. It was the break of a lifetime for eighteen-year-old Rick, and the next two years, Rick and Kim would produce live boxing and wrestling programs all over the east coast.

Cable television was gaining ground quickly in the broadcast market, and Christian television programming was blossoming. Bigger networks were stepping in to fill the markets that previously belonged to smaller stations, and small stations like the Jesus Is Lord Television Network simply couldn't compete with the deeper pockets of the cable newcomers. Richard and Rick knew that the time had come to sell the station, and Rick turned his attention to regional television production.

His life was rich and fulfilling in so many ways, and he knew that God was the force behind every blessing that came his way. Still, he had yet to find someone to share his life with. As Rick nursed a broken heart from a relationship that had soured, the twenty-year-old wondered when he would find the woman God wanted him to marry.

The family had become friends with Pat and Vicki, a couple who not only attended the same church, but also lived in the same housing development. Each year, Pat's younger sister Stephanie would travel from her home in England to stay with them. While visiting, Pat's sister enjoyed spending much of her time working at a horse farm in nearby Pennsylvania. This time around, Pat and Vicki were interested in seeing her make some two-legged friends instead of spending all her time with four-legged ones. After gaining Carmelita's approval, Vicki asked Rick if he would be willing to take her sister-in-law around and show her some of the sights of the area.

"I tell you what," he responded. "I'll not only show her around, I'll drive you to the airport to pick her up."

Vicki was surprised by the offer, and Rick was just as surprised to hear the words come out of his mouth. With Vicki there, he would have the chance to find out if he had anything in common with this girl, and figured that he could always make up an excuse if he didn't want to spend time showing her around the town.

They arrived at Philadelphia International Airport on a June weekend, and Rick would never forget the first time he caught a glimpse of Stephanie as she walked down the ramp toward them. She wore a black blouse and a simple skirt, and her brown eyes sparkled with warmth and sincerity. A feeling that he had never known before came over him. Rick knew that if there was such a thing as love at first sight, he was experiencing it. The ride from the airport to Pat and Vicki's home stretched into dinner, and when he didn't arrive home until eleven o'clock that night, Carmelita suspected that the meeting had gone well.

Stephanie was passionate about horses. Rick, on the other hand, had never even been horseback riding before, but readily volunteered to go riding with her. The young couple crammed the two-week visit with every activity imaginable; Rick took her to the Delaware State Fair and to Atlantic City for an ESPN broadcast.

They talked for hours and Rick felt as if he had found a best friend. The fact that she took his breath away was just icing on the cake.

By the end of Stephanie's two-week stay, they both knew something was happening, but also knew that they had numerous obstacles between them. Her life was in England, where she had a good-paying job as a word processor for a major company. His life was here, where he was enjoying the ground-floor opportunity of a lifetime with cable network television production. As he took her to the airport for her return flight home, he felt as if he was breaking off a piece of his heart and sending it away indefinitely. Her absence didn't just leave a hole in his heart; it took a piece of his with her.

They stood at the airport, ecstatic to have found each other but crushed to say goodbye. As her flight was called, they looked at one another, tracing every detail of one another's face into their memory to be savored later. Rick handed Stephanie a card he had bought; she handed him one in return. And then, as magically and as quickly as she had appeared in his life, she was disappearing through the doorway that led to her plane.

Rick carried Stephanie with him in his heart, thinking of her the moment he opened his eyes and seeing her in his mind as he fell asleep at night. She was unlike anyone he had ever known before, and she inspired music and poetry within him that he could not contain. Each night, when the rest of the house had fallen asleep, Rick would go to the church with his cassette recorder and record songs he had written for her. Every morning, he would put a new tape in the mail to her, determined that she would get something new from him every day.

Stephanie was not a musician, but she loved music nearly as much as Rick did. In lieu of composing music, she would tape songs that made her think about him and send them to Rick. Wrapped around each of their letters were lengthy, heartfelt dissertations about their feelings, hopes and dreams. Despite the distance, they were able to continue fanning the spark that had been ignited between them in June, and they dreamed of a time when they could be together again.

Long-distance telephone calls were still extremely expensive, and they rationed themselves to one brief phone call each week. In October, it was Stephanie who called Rick with news that filled him with joy.

She was coming back to Delaware with her father, she explained, and they would be able to see one another. She would be staying indefinitely.

Rick was ecstatic. They had not discussed marriage, but he knew that this was the woman he wanted to spend the rest of his life with. It was much too soon to ask for her hand, but something unspoken between them told him it would happen. What he didn't know at that moment was that Stephanie also knew they would spend the rest of their lives together; her trip back to Delaware was more than just a casual getaway.

Stephanie had been unable to shake thoughts of Rick, and the longer she was separated from him, the more her desire to be with him grew. Before she boarded the plane to return to Delaware, she had sold all of her personal belongings – including her beloved horses – knowing that she would be marrying Rick and living the rest of her life with him in the United States.

Their courtship evolved over the next few months. As winter set in, Stephanie would run from her brother's home to Rick's parents' house, waking Rick in the morning hours by tossing snowballs at his bedroom window. It was such a delight for Rick to look out and see her standing, as he longed to wake up next to her. On December 7, 1979, he took steps toward making that dream a reality. As they sat in the basement of his parent's home, Rick got up the courage to ask the question that had been on his mind for the past few months. As he got down on one knee, Vince suddenly burst down the stairs, completely oblivious to what was about to happen. Rick stood and asked Vince to give him some privacy. As his little brother disappeared back upstairs, Rick returned to his knee and asked Stephanie to marry him. The answer was, of course, an unhesitating affirmative.

Initially the couple kept the engagement quiet, knowing that a chorus of warnings from well-meaning family members was inevitable. Stephanie's father, who was staying in the United States through the end of the year, met with Rick at a Howard Johnson's in Delaware to express his concern. No one doubted the love and desire between the two twenty-year-olds, but older family members offered numerous warnings about their youthfulness and the need to "get to know one another better."

The warnings fell on deaf ears. Rick and Stephanie knew that the love they had was genuine, and nothing was going to stop them from becoming man and wife. Realizing that the couple was willing to move heaven and earth to make their marriage happen, the warnings from family members soon turned to heartfelt wishes for happiness.

In order for Stephanie to marry Rick, she had to complete paperwork and file it in London. The idea of separating from his beloved fiancée again was wrenching, but Rick knew the split would be brief and temporary. They completed all the documents they could in the United States, then Stephanie flew back to London late in January for the final filing of the documents. Both of them were so excited, knowing this paperwork was the only thing standing between the two of them and matrimonial bliss. Rick was surprised when Stephanie called the following day.

Sobbing into the phone, Stephanie told Rick that the paperwork they had submitted had never been received, and that all of the documentation they had worked so hard to complete was missing. As a result, not only was she unable to complete filing for their marriage to be approved, she also was unable to return to the United States.

Rick was stunned. This couldn't be happening! He knew that he would find a way to get her back to the states. He told Stephanie he would make some phone calls. As soon as they told one another goodbye, he immediately picked up the phone and began dialing.

His calls yielded plenty of sympathetic responses, but no real assistance. Still, Rick kept dialing. His persistence finally landed him on the other end of a phone call with a Delaware congressman.

He explained his dilemma, and the urgency in his voice spoke to his determination to get his bride back to Delaware.

The congressman agreed to meet. Rick gave an impassioned presentation of the facts that had put he and Stephanie in this dilemma. Sympathetic to the cause of young, determined love, the congressman told Rick to tell Stephanie to get on that plane and come home; when she arrived in customs, he had agents waiting to escort her from the airport on a special pass. He even arranged for the couple to be able to submit their documentation to England after the marriage had taken place.

Rick and Stephanie set their wedding date for April 27, 1980 – the same day as Richard and Carmelita's anniversary. Inside the Holy Family Catholic Church, with their family and friends watching, Father Michael Angeloni led Rick and Stephanie through their vows. In true Silanskas style, the ceremony contained plenty of music. After a quick reception, a limousine whisked the newlyweds away to their hotel in Philadelphia. They would spend their first night together in Philadelphia, then fly to Florida for their honeymoon the following morning.

Rick held Stephanie in his arms as the limousine made the hour-long trek to their hotel. He was so happy to have her as his wife and could not believe they were finally on their own. It was a new beginning for them, the chance to begin a life that was open to any possibility they could dream of.

In their hotel room, Rick gazed at his new bride and marveled at how beautiful she was. As he kissed her, the phone rang. Startled, Rick answered it.

"Did you forget something, son?"

Rick was surprised to hear Richard's voice on the other end of the line, and wasn't necessarily in the mood for conversation.

"Uh, no, I don't think so…" Rick replied, puzzled.

"What about your wallet?"

Rick felt a wave of disbelief washing over him as he checked his pants pocket. He had changed out of his tuxedo at the church – and had somehow left his wallet behind! All of his money, their airline tickets, everything they needed beyond each other, was in his wallet, which now was an hour away in the hands and home of his parents.

Carmelita took the phone. "Rick, why don't you wait for us in the lobby. We can drive up there. We'll be there in an hour."

Rick couldn't believe this was happening. He looked at his beautiful bride.

"Put dad back on the phone, please, Mom…"

Richard's voice reassured his son even before Rick had uttered a word.

"Don't worry about it, son. We'll leave it in an envelope at the front desk."

Rick breathed a sigh of relief. It was an auspicious start to the honeymoon, and the next morning he and Stephanie made the mercifully uneventful flight to Florida. Rick loved amusement parks and longed to work at Walt Disney Studios, and Stephanie had never been to Disney World. Rick took her to the places he had visited and fallen in love with as a child on family vacations. Their honeymoon was punctuated by mishaps that they would later laugh about; their first hotel had, in the week since Rick made the reservation, decided to renovate its honeymoon suite. Not only did the suite no longer exist, but they were serenaded by the sound of construction in a lesser quality room.

The second hotel they visited had a honeymoon suite, but also had an overeager maid who burst in on the couple and insisted she could "clean around them." Horrified, Rick insisted the maid leave while Stephanie hid beneath the sheets. By the time they arrived at their third destination, Rick was beginning to wonder if their honeymoon would ever afford them some privacy. Just half an hour after they checked in, the phone rang, and an insistent salesman tried to convince them to take a thirty-minute visit to his nearby resort in exchange for a new set of luggage.

"No, thank you, but we're really not interested," Rick told him, explaining they were on their honeymoon and had no interest in buying anything. The salesman later approached them in the hotel parking lot, and Rick now was growing impatient. He firmly but politely told the man they were not interested and asked him not to bother them further.

Rick and Stephanie stayed out late that night, enjoying the sights and sounds of Orlando. Exhausted from the late night and all the activities of the week, they placed the "Do not disturb" sign on the door and decided to sleep in. When the phone rang the next morning Rick refused to answer it, assuming it was the pesky, persistent timeshare salesman.

Their peaceful slumber was short-lived. Less than an hour later, Rick and Stephanie were roused from bed by fists pounding on the door, followed by the command, "Police! Open up!" Scrambling for his robe, Rick answered the door and found a concerned pair of officers standing with the hotel manager. They had received an anonymous tip from an "acquaintance," saying he hadn't heard from the couple and feared that they had committed suicide inside the hotel room.

Rick shook his head in disbelief, knowing their persistent salesman was likely the culprit behind the phone call. He and Stephanie would later laugh about the mishaps that followed their honeymoon, but they had to admit that it made for a memorable first vacation.

The more time they spent in Florida, the more determined Rick was to move there. He even managed to get a job interview with one of the attractions in Orlando, but was unable to land a job so the newlyweds returned to Delaware to begin their new life together.

Rick did land a new job, but it was as producer, salesman and on-air personality for WSER in Elkton, where he had landed his first job at the age of sixteen. He thrived in the environment, adding sales to his list of duties and becoming the station's top salesman. In less than a year, Rick landed a job as promotions director with the CBS affiliate WBOC in Laurel, Maryland. The position required that the new couple move away from their close-knit family environment. It was an unprecedented move; not only had Rick married and moved out of the house, but now he was moving two hours away! The situation took some explaining before it gained his parents' acceptance. But soon, he and Stephanie had settled into a routine;

she took a job with Blue Cross Blue Shield, and Rick entrenched himself in television. He and Stephanie bought a small house, then just when it seemed that life could not get any richer for them, they learned that Stephanie was pregnant with their first child.

As much as he and Stephanie loved their time alone together, they were ecstatic at the prospect of beginning a new chapter in their lives. Maria was born on April 6, 1982, in Salisbury, Maryland. The young couple reveled in their new role as parents. At the same time, Rick's desire to move to Florida intensified. He dreamed of working for Walt Disney, and began applying at television stations in the area. He was thrilled when he landed a position doing promotions for a central Florida station.

The announcement of their impending move had a somewhat unexpected effect on the rest of his family: They all instantly liked the idea and followed the young couple to the Sunshine State just a few months later. Rick and Stephanie bought a small home in Fruitland Park, and he settled into his job at Channel 55 in Leesburg.

As much as he loved his work in television, Rick frequently found himself frustrated by the limits of his environment. The work was done primarily by contractors. He found that the hired hands who were there to do a job often lacked any personal interest in the project. It was rare to find someone who could capture his vision on tape. Rick began dreaming of a production company that would not compromise its quality and could provide all the services needed beneath one umbrella. It was the beginning of what would become DreamVision. Although it would take a few years to blossom from the seed of an idea into a business, Rick already knew his television experiences were preparing him for a much larger endeavor.

Rick also continued growing his family. His first son, Tony, was born in 1984, followed three years later by Jessica. Their fourth child, Andrew, came along in 1990, evenly dividing the boys-to-girl ratio of the household.

In his children, Rick found a new love for life and a renewed appreciation for Stephanie. He was the dreaming idealist; she was the pragmatic realist who brought him back to earth. Beyond what she did to keep Rick's feet on the ground, she somehow managed to be a firm but nurturing parent. They instilled their children with the Biblical principles she and Rick embraced, and Stephanie worked hard to be not just a loving mother but an exemplary role model for their children.

Rick was amazed at how his children grew into extensions of his own life. While each one of them had their own, distinct personalities, they also had some of Rick's specific characteristics. Maria inherited Rick's fascination with and passion for children, something that would later lead her into the field of education. Tony loved movies from the moment he first saw them, and that would later draw him into the film industry. Jessica's love for the arts manifested itself in a natural ability and affinity for dance. Little Andrew had his father's love of music and also shared Rick's passion for movies.

It was Rick's own love of music that often kept him from the children he loved so dearly. He began working at nights in an effort both to earn extra money and to further his musical career. After working a full day at the television station, Rick would head to Old Town, a tourist attraction near DisneyWorld, where he had a one-man show. He performed three shows a night, five times a week, playing classic rock hits. In the mornings, he would drive the children to school, giving him a little bit of time to spend with them and providing Stephanie with a much-needed break. Once a week, Stephanie loaded the children into the car and made the drive to Orlando, stopping at a restaurant where, on Tuesday nights, children ate for free before taking them to see their father perform his show.

On a whim, Rick began doing a medley of Elvis songs to close out his show. His lifelong fascination with The King had morphed into the show's finale, with Rick slipping off stage to quickly change into a white Elvis-style jumpsuit before coming out to finish his set.

Although it was not exactly Broadway, Rick enjoyed performing his show. The crowds were always appreciative and he enjoyed the thrill of playing in front of a live audience. He had been performing the show for about three years when Old Town management decided to bring in a special act for Thanksgiving Week. The specialty circus act was called The Wheel of Death. It featured a trapeze artist who performed in a circular wire wheel high above the stage. For the show's finale, the artist would leap on top of the wheel and run, sending the wheel spinning faster and faster before he dismounted and ran into the audience.

Rick's role was to play live music while the trapeze artist performed. At rehearsals, the show's producers were very specific in their instructions to Rick: When the trapeze artist dismounted, Rick was to remain seated. The wire wheel was at the end of a forty-foot pole; providing the counterbalance to the wheel was a five-hundred-pound weight. The weight would be swung to the ground immediately following the trapeze artist's dismount, and for Rick's own safety, he was not to move from his piano bench until the weight that kept the wheel balanced had been lowered to the ground. It was a tight space, and the slightest deviation from routine could be dangerous at best.

Rick wasn't particularly excited about sharing his stage with another act, but the crowd was receiving it well. He awoke on Friday morning, the day after Thanksgiving, still basking in the glow of the big family celebration the day before. He was tired and did not want to go to work, but also knew that this would be one of the largest weekends of the year as the holiday season officially began.

It was around 8:10 p.m. when the first show came to a close, and it had gone smoothly, although Rick could tell he was tired and wasn't playing with the same heartfelt joy he usually brought to the stage. As usual, the trapeze artist dismounted and disappeared into the crowd amongst thunderous applause. Weary and forgetting the instruction not to move, Rick instinctively rose and turned to walk to the back of the stage. As the five-hundred-pound weight came swinging from the scaffolding above the stage, its momentum lifted Rick from the ground and threw him across the stage. Blackness filled his head and he struggled to understand what had just happened to him. As he put his hands to his head, he could feel the blood that covered his face, and then, in horror, realized he was able to slip his fingers inside his own forehead.

The show manager and workers helped him to the bathroom, where Rick collapsed on the floor. He opened his eyes and could see the trapeze artist cradling Rick's head in his hands, begging Rick to forgive him. The owner of the Old Town attraction stood over him, the look of horror unshielded by the tears that ran from his eyes.

As soon as the ambulance arrived, paramedics bandaged Rick's head and started an IV drip. They wanted to call his wife and he begged them not to, afraid they would scare Stephanie, who was home alone with the children. Ignoring his pleas, they loaded him into the ambulance and Rick could hear the sirens wailing as they rushed him to the hospital in Kissimmee. He could hear the paramedics talking to him and he did his best to respond. Rick realized that they were growing more and more distant from him, and even though he could hear what they were saying, he was no longer able to respond to them.

"We're losing him," Rick heard one of them say. He was aware of the ambulance pulling over to the side of the road. He wanted to reassure them that he was fine. Rick felt a kind of peaceful happiness that he had never known before, a blissful, loving sense of warmth. The faces of the paramedics faded and were replaced by the most brilliant, perfect light he had ever seen. With each breath, he felt a deeper sense of peace and the light seemed to grow even brighter and warmer.

In an instant, Rick felt a giant force of suction pulling him away from the light and he suddenly found himself looking at the paramedics as they unloaded the gurney from the ambulance. He closed his eyes once again and did not open them again until he felt Stephanie's hand on top of his.

Rick opened his eyes. She was standing over him, her eyes a combination of love and terror. He looked at those beautiful brown eyes staring intently at him and saw the love and concern that filled them. Rick couldn't imagine anything better than waking up with those eyes looking at him.

The doctor joined them in the room just as Rick was becoming aware of his surroundings.

"Someone must want your husband to be here, Mrs. Silanskas," he began, handing Stephanie a CAT scan. The doctor explained that, had the point of impact to Rick's head occurred just one-tenth of a centimeter in either direction, he would have been killed instantly. The words were chilling and also served as a strong reminder of God's ever-present protection in their lives. Rick knew God had a plan and a purpose for him. He knew that there was much in his life still to be accomplished.

After a slow recuperation, Rick returned briefly to the show at Old Town, but by then his passion for the performance was gone. He knew that he had much greater things to do in his life, and for the rest of his life, the scar on the side of his head would remind Rick that God was not finished with him.

Chapter Eight

Rick's early plan to develop a full-service television studio and production company had come to fruition by the mid-eighties, first as a part-time side venture and then growing into a full-time multi-faceted business. Because the business was a dream or vision that became reality, and its purpose was to make reality from the dreams or visions of others, Rick chose the name DreamVision Studios.

Richard joined his son, working in the administrative end of the business. Vince, meanwhile, had landed a position with Walt Disney/MGM Studios, where he was stage manager and production manager. He worked with Rick on several projects before deciding to leave Disney and join Rick and Richard full-time. The company did well, creating television commercials, jingles and documentaries for clients throughout central Florida. Rick won numerous awards, including being the recipient of the National Telly Award multiple times for his original scores.

With Vince on board, they began producing large-scale fireworks shows that consisted of Rick's original music score set to a live fireworks production for special events, corporations and, of course, the holidays.

Everything Rick had planned for the studio was coming to fruition. The state-of-the-art facility became a new vehicle for Rick to pursue all of his interests. He was able to combine his love for film, television and music under one roof, and he reveled in his work.

Following his passion allowed Rick to provide nicely for his family. By the time the eighties drew to a close, they owned a large spread in Lady Lake, Florida, and Rick was finally able to replace the beloved horses Stephanie had sold so many years earlier in England to come start her life with him. Opportunities continued coming their way. In 1997 Rick was given the opportunity to score a motion picture. Although the movie did not do well at the box office, the score garnered praise from critics and, soon after the movie's release, Rick was invited to perform at the Hard Rock Live Theater in Orlando.

To his surprise, more than two thousand people filled the room that night. The concert was filmed and became a television special that aired on the Bravo International Network. "Rick Silanskas In Concert" was packaged in a two-hour block with another concert by the golden-throated Italian singing sensation Andrea Bocelli. The television special aired in twenty-one countries, and Rick suddenly found himself getting airplay in South America and Central America.

Although his ability at the piano was unmistakable, it was the way Rick related to his audience that seemed to most win them over. Because every song he played was inspired by some event that occurred in his life, he took time between songs and offered brief, entertaining vignettes of his life. His easy-going demeanor made audiences open to both his words and music, and almost overnight Rick found himself becoming popular.

Rick had recorded four CDs, but didn't have a distributor for his music. He sold them at live performances or on the Internet, and shortly after his television special aired on Bravo, he began working in earnest to push his music career. Rick had been given just a small taste of what he had so adored all his life; he loved being on the stage and performing in front of a packed, appreciative house.

His push for musical success began to climb. He was invited to places such as Lima, Peru, Buenes Aires and Santiago, Chile, where fans had seen his live television performance and wanted now to hear him in person. In Peru, he and Stephanie were shocked to find hordes of people awaiting their arrival at the airport. The Peruvian version of "People" magazine, called "Gente," dedicated three consecutive cover stories to Rick and dubbed him "The Ambassador of Romance." He did countless radio interviews and, by the time he returned to the states, he also had picked up an endorsement from Bosendorfer grand pianos in Austria. Everything that Rick once had dreamed of now seemed to be on the verge of coming true. It looked as if stardom was now inevitable.

Rick traveled to England with Stephanie, combining business with pleasure as they visited the spots where Stephanie had spent her childhood. Rick was there to promote his music, but it was also a delight to spend time in Stephanie's homeland. Before the couple returned home, Rick was invited to present his work to the Royal Family at Buckingham Palace. Even Stephanie's buttoned-down family was obviously impressed at the opportunity.

They arrived at Buckingham Palace on the appointed day, and both of them found themselves a bit breathless with anticipation. Walking across the courtyard, Rick whispered to Stephanie, "Walk real slow. We're never going to get the chance to do this again!"

It was an event just to walk across the courtyard to the palace, while onlookers wondered who they were and what they had done to be given access to the Buckingham Palace. They met with the queen's lady in waiting, who presented them with a letter from the Royal Family. Rick, in turn, presented her with his music as a gift for the family.

Backtracking their steps across the courtyard, Rick felt grateful and overwhelmed by the way his career was progressing. Best of all, he knew that this was simply the beginning.

To close out the first year of the new millennium, Rick was invited to participate in the Hollywood Christmas Parade in Los Angeles, California. He had now fully embraced his Ambassador of Romance persona, right down to the sunglasses and leather pants. He rode on the third float, playing a Bosendorfer piano for the crowd as the parade made its way down the street. In the Green Room, alongside other celebrities like Beau Bridges, Erik Estrada and the cast of the hit television show "7th Heaven," Rick felt like he was entering a new phase of his career. The momentum was incredible. As 2001 dawned, Rick's excitement over his flowering career could not be contained. He had begun working with a composer out of

Nashville named Don Marsh, who was able to take Rick's musical visions and arrange them into lush, beautifully orchestrated pieces. Even though Rick had never learned how to sight-read music, he was able to hear entire orchestrations in his head.

Thanks to the equipment he had furnished DreamVision with, he was able to sit at a keyboard and record his compositions as he wrote. Rick would write the score for each section of an orchestra, then give Don the recording and let him transform them into arrangements. The partnership was a strong and mutually beneficial one, and Rick knew that they had been brought together for a specific reason.

It was time for him to take his music and his show to the next level. He was ready for live audiences and a regular gig as the Ambassador of Romance. Rick was ready to break out into the starring role he had been born to play, and he knew what he needed to do to take it to the next level.

It was time to go to Vegas!

Rick's charismatic personality and audience-friendly musical journey seemed like a natural fit for the crowds that swarm the Vegas strip. He could capitalize upon his "Ambassador of Romance" persona and do in Vegas what he had done at the Hard Rock Live. He was determined to become a headliner in Vegas. He and Vince began pouring much of their energy into making that show a reality.

Persistence and networking paid off, as they booked four shows at the Imperial Palace in September and October. Rick was thrilled about what the show would do for his career; he and Vince envisioned hugely successful nights that would lead to an extended invitation for an ongoing act. That was all Rick needed for his future as a successful artist to be secured, and they pursued it with the same determination that had brought them this far.

As the date approached, the marketing blitz reached a feverish pitch. Billboards along the Vegas strip told of the coming visit from the Ambassador of Romance, and television commercials gave audiences a small taste of what to expect. They covered all the bases, doing the advance media work needed to fill the seats.

Everything about this new direction seemed destined to succeed. Rick had been music director at his church for several years now, and while he continued in that role, his mind was focused more on preparing for his Vegas act. He knew he could win over the crowds in Vegas, and he knew of nothing that could stop him.

Rick dropped his children off at school as usual on the morning of September 11, 2001, then headed to his office in Winter Garden. It was about 8:40 a.m. when Stephanie called.

"Turn on the television, right away," she told him, her voice sharp with alarm. "Something terrible has happened."

Her voice was filled with something Rick couldn't describe and had never heard before. He turned on a television in the DreamVision offices and watched in horror as the terrorist attacks on the United States unfolded. Rick was dumbfounded, not able to believe what he was seeing. As the coverage of the plane hitting the Pentagon came on the air, Rick became panic-stricken. He felt vulnerable in a way he could not explain and all he wanted to do was return to the safety and solace of his home, which was forty-five minutes away.

Rick listened to the news reports on the radio as he drove home, tears streaming down his face. His mission and music now seemed so insignificant in light of all that was taking place and, for the first time in his life, the music in Rick's head went silent. He talked to Vince, who was setting up equipment for the first of two shows Rick was supposed to perform beginning that night. They had scheduled a dress rehearsal of sorts for Rick's Vegas show, knowing that the local audiences loved Rick's performances and the turnout would be good. The two shows were scheduled for September 11 and 12, and the brothers immediately agreed that the performances must be cancelled.

The cancellations of the shows drew an unexpected response, as many of the evening's ticket holders called and were disappointed that the show would not go on as planned. By the morning of September 12, the manager of the facility hosting the show had contacted Vince, requesting that the evening's show go on as planned.

"People are calling in, saying they need this," she explained to Vince. "I think it's important for Rick to be here tonight."

Rick's performance was more thoughtful than usual, and while the tone would not be considered somber, it definitely was shadowed by the events of the day before. Like a close-knit family gathering around a piano singing beloved songs after a funeral, the crowd bonded with Rick and his music in an exceptional way. It was a touching experience, and even though Rick's heart wasn't in his performance, he connected with his audience that night in a way that only tragedy allows.

Like many of the people in the days following the attacks, Rick spent a great deal of time feeling dazed and disoriented, unsure of what was happening in the world that once felt so safe. Where once his life was filled with music, he now felt no connection to the melodies that seemed to flow through his veins. Instead of listening to CDs in his car, Rick found himself glued to the news channels. He was despondent and reflective, feeling a dark sadness that nothing seemed to alleviate. Even in church, he had difficulty playing his music without tearing up or breaking down in tears.

Opening night on the Vegas strip was rapidly approaching, and Rick now had little passion for what had, just days earlier, entirely consumed him. The show would have a live eight-piece band backing Rick and would include all the whistles and bells it needed to be a hit. Rick couldn't find it within himself to care.

The dark days that followed September 11 prompted many hotels and concert venues to cancel their shows, but at the Imperial Palace, the Rick Silanskas show was going to proceed as planned. They prepared for the September 23 opening night, but Rick still felt flat inside. He knew he could pull it out once he hit the stage, knew that it was possible to turn it on like a faucet and make the show happen.

From his spot in the production booth that night, Vince could tell Rick wasn't himself from the moment Rick walked on stage. He went through the act, technically flawless but somehow removed from his audience. The audience was a disappointing turnout as well; few people were turning out in the wake of the tragic events that had occurred, and it was evident that neither performer nor audience was really enthralled by what was happening on stage that night.

Rick left the stage that night feeling defeated and embarrassed. He was not entirely surprised when the general manager of the Palace told Rick he was canceling the contract; Rick would not need to return for the remaining three scheduled shows.

It was a milestone in his career, but certainly not the one Rick had been anticipating. He returned to his home in Florida, feeling humiliated and depressed. Despondent, Rick submerged deep within himself.

The weeks that followed were dark and difficult, not just for Rick, but for all of those who loved him. He fell into a dark hole somewhere deep inside his heart, seemingly unable to crawl out of it. Instead of going to work, he would drive to a secluded park and sit for hours, wondering what he had done with the gift God had given him.

Everything about the past few years had been selfish and wrong, he now believed.

"Look at where you are and what you're doing and for what reason," he would berate himself, wondering what it all meant. He beat himself up unmercifully, knowing that he had failed because he had been pursuing fame rather than trying to serve God with his talents. He felt like an ungrateful child who had been given a beautiful gift and, instead of treasuring it, chose to tear it apart.

He had wanted to become a superstar, and for the life of him, Rick could not explain why. Did he simply want to hear people scream his name and buy his records? Was it just his love of the applause? It all seemed so selfish, so unimportant now, and he didn't know what to do next. He didn't want to play music; if fact, he did not even want to hear it. He had no idea of where to go from here and couldn't even say what it was that he wanted to do.

Stephanie was one of the few people who could reach Rick by phone. He refused most calls. People he knew both through church and business began growing concerned about him. As the days dragged into weeks, it seemed that Rick's state grew more despondent. Finally, his good friend and mentor Don Marsh called him from Nashville. Don knew this was a difficult time, but he had never seen Rick in such great despair. He called Rick on a Wednesday morning in mid-October.

"Rick, I know you're having a difficult time, but you really need to write music," he said. Rick could not have disagreed with him more.

"Just listen to me. I want to fax you something. You've got to read it. It needs music."

The fax that came across Rick's machine moments later struck a chord in his heart that had laid dormant for several weeks. The poem was a touching and inspirational piece of work by a Marine named Father Dennis O'Brien. It spoke to the sacrifices made by soldiers, and as Rick read it he was moved to tears.

Rick always had a strong respect for the armed forces and the men and women who served in the military, but he had never truly considered the magnitude of their service. The poem reached deep inside of him, moving him in such a way that he knew what needed to be done next.

"I'm going to the studio tonight," he informed Stephanie, who was simultaneously surprised and pleased by his words. Rick arrived at the studio after everyone had left for the day. He sat at the keyboard, looking at it with an uncomfortable weight in his heart. His hands felt as heavy as rock, and he didn't know how he could take the faint sounds he heard in his head and transform them into notes.

Rick was overcome with painful remorse, and as he sat at the keyboard he began to sob. He felt disgusted with himself, annoyed that he had been given such magnificent blessings from God, but had not used them in the best way possible. He realized that, during the course of his life, he had always included God in his life, but he had allowed so many things to come between them in recent years. Rick had turned up the volume of his life so loudly that he could no longer hear the still, small voice of an all-powerful God.

"God," he prayed. "If you will give me my gift back, I promise always to use it for you."

His hand lightly touched the keyboard in front of him. He sat there, frozen for a few minutes and it seemed as if the cold distance between Rick and his music was being bridged as he sat there. The music began playing in his head and he couldn't transfer it to the keys quickly enough. It wasn't just a song or melody, as he had written before; it was an entire symphony. Rick wrote "The American Freedom Suite," a symphony in four movements that chronicled the feelings he had beginning the moment he had turned on the television on September 11. The music walked through his despair and pain, ending with "A New Freedom," which projected the hope he felt as he returned to God's love.

The music poured out of him and once the symphony was completed, he composed music to accompany the poem Don had sent to him. His mind was still filled with music, and he wrote a hopeful, patriotic number called "I Believe in America." Finally, as morning broke over the Orlando skyline, Rick composed what would become a beautiful finale to his next album, simply titled "Remembrance."

He walked from the studio before anyone else arrived, feeling physically and mentally drained but spiritually renewed. Rick had a revitalized sense of purpose. He was ready to return to his music the way that God wanted it to be played.

Less than a week later, over lunch with a friend from an Orlando radio station, Rick casually mentioned what he had been working on. She immediately jumped at the chance to hear the music, and suggested that Rick make a recording that could be presented to the nation's soldiers. Rick was surprised by her response; he hadn't thought of the symphony as a commercial venture or even something for public display. He had written it as an emotional release, a way to cry out over all the events that had taken place in the past few months, a way to mourn the wounds inflicted on the nation's psyche on the morning of September 11. It was as if his tears and blood had flowed right into the keyboard to compose the music; Rick felt in many ways that he had simply been the conduit that transcribed the notes.

Rick recorded the songs he had written, then gave it to his friend at the radio station. As soon as station executives heard the music, WDBO-AM radio scheduled the symphony's world premiere at the Savannah Center for the Performing Arts in The Villages, Florida. The special invitation-only event brought together more than one thousand veterans who had served the country in every war, as well as their family members. As Rick walked onto the stage on a balmy night in early December, he was overwhelmed by what he saw: Aged veterans in wheelchairs shared the room with fresh-faced young soldiers on their way to Afghanistan. Rick was joined on stage by a one hundred-piece symphony, conducted by Don Marsh, and a two hundred-voice choir. Rick found himself completely overwhelmed by the way the words and music collided, filling the hall. He sat at the piano, feeling the music flow through him, knowing that he was again using his gifts in the way God had intended them to be used.

By the end of the evening, Rick knew a subtle but powerful change had occurred inside of him. It wasn't about what Rick wanted anymore, it was about the gift God had given him and the way he would use it.

The concert was broadcast on Armed Forces Radio. DreamVision recorded the live broadcast to produce the CD, "The American Freedom Suite," which they made available on a web site called www.RemembertheSoldier.com. Rick's passion and priorities had shifted. As America closed out one of the most difficult years in its history, Rick felt grateful that, despite some very hard lessons, he had emerged stronger. He knew now he was willing to follow whatever path God wanted him to walk down.

The Silanskas family celebrated Christmas with its traditional fanfare, and Rick reveled in the festivities with a heightened sense of awareness. No longer concerned about his success or becoming a superstar, Rick knew he was ready to turn his attention back to what was truly important.

Over the next two months, subtle changes started slipping into Rick's life and, while not always noticed by him, those around Rick took note. At first, those changes were as imperceptible as the ones that had led him away from his walk with the Lord to begin with. He became more focused and aware of those around him. His relationship with Stephanie had always been good, but now Rick felt a renewed passion and dedication to his wife. Rick began studying the scriptures more diligently. At a Christian convention in February 2002, he picked up some videos by a man named Leonardo DeFilippis. A gifted actor and producer, Leonardo had made a series of tapes featuring his one-man portrayals of different figures from the Bible. At home, Rick watched the video "John of the Cross," Leonardo's depiction of St. John of the Cross, who died in 1591 at the age of forty-nine. St. John had been intent on becoming so close to Christ that, upon his death, his spiritual state would be the same as it had been on earth. He spent tremendous periods of time in prayer, and when he spoke out against the worldly activities of the others in his brotherhood, he was kidnapped and persecuted.

Rick was transfixed and touched by the story. He wanted his life to be that exemplary, although he knew he could never come close. Still, he wanted to try. Rick begged God to tear down the structure of his life and begin rebuilding Rick, brick by brick.

Rick went to the church where he served as music minister. He knelt before the altar, feeling unworthy of God's grace and ashamed for all the times he had put himself first in his life. He knew now that being a Christian wasn't about appearances or knowing what words to say at the right time; it was about dedicating everything that he did, every moment of the day, to the service of God.

His heart felt as if it would burst. Rick felt such gratitude for all he had been given, and such shame for all he had squandered.

"God, here…take my music, my dreams, my plans and my visions," he begged, mentally handing over everything he had.

"I give you my fatherhood and my husbandship. Everything that I am, I give it back to you. Take it and fill me with your dreams and your visions and your love, because I know that it's going to be a whole lot better than anything I can plan for myself."

He was tired of trying to do it himself, tired of trying to do things his way. The volume that he had turned up so loudly over the past few years was now turned back down, and Rick began to listen. His love of life seemed to multiply each day, and the subtle but powerful changes began transforming him from deep inside.

By summertime, Rick was a changed man. He was more focused at work and his children delighted in the new relationship they were enjoying with their father. Rick woke up each day, grateful for all that he had been given and eager to see what new opportunities awaited him.

Rick and Stephanie began to talk about their future together. Tony and Maria now were both in college, and before long Jessica and Andrew would follow them out the door and on to their adult lives. It would be a new chapter for them, a revisiting of that cherished time when they had first met - just the two of them.

So much had changed since then, but their love for one another had only deepened with time. Rick knew that Stephanie had sacrificed everything for him. From the time she sold all her worldly belongings to the way she daily held the family together, he felt as if she had been the most remarkable woman he had ever known. He didn't know how he would have made it through his life without her, and he was thankful he didn't have to dwell on that thought. For all she had done through the years, he wanted to make it up to her, make their years alone together as spectacular as the few years they shared before the children came along.

Rick had an excitement for the future that could not be contained. He knew that his life was changing, and although he wasn't sure where it was going to lead him, Rick was not concerned about it. He knew that he was no longer in charge; he had surrendered everything to God. All he had to do now was simply listen and obey. There was no way Rick could have known that what God was about to show him would change his whole life completely.

Chapter Nine

None of the changes in Rick's life gave any foreshadowing of the dream that changed his life on December 23, 2002. Rick knew that God was speaking to him, telling him that this little girl was waiting for him. He could feel it in his heart, but could do nothing to make his search for her move more quickly.

Ever since the night of that dream, Rick's prayers had taken on an urgent tone, an appeal from one father to another. He had such a longing in his heart, an ache to hold that baby in his arms once again. Rick had spent hours pleading with God to give him the strength to continue searching for that little girl. At that moment in time, it seemed quite likely to Rick that God was the only one who could understand what he was going through.

Even in the midst of other people, Rick felt lonesome, his heart empty with a hole that he knew could only be filled by the little brown-eyed child in the dream. He had begged God to hear his prayers, begged God to watch over that little girl and bring her into Rick's arms once again.

Every day Rick sat down at his computer, painfully going through the heart-wrenching activity of searching the web site, looking for his little girl. The site filled with pictures of Russian orphans had not been modified or updated during the three weeks he had monitored it, but he continued looking. As he sat before his computer on the morning of January 18, 2003, he felt a certainty that God had heard his prayers.

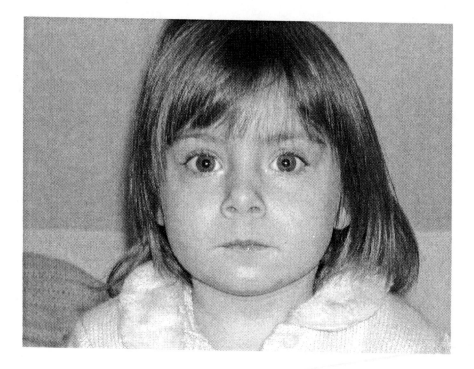

Nadia as found

As soon as Stephanie had informed him that they were approved for international adoption, he checked the site once again. At first, it was the same as it had been moments earlier when Rick checked it. Then, right before his eyes, the page reloaded. It had been updated to add one more child to the site. He clicked on the appropriate page and watched in awe as the information appeared on the screen.

The new child was a female. Two and a half years old. By the name of Nadezchda.

The information appeared succinctly, a clinical listing of facts. And then, as Rick stared in amazement at the computer screen, the picture appeared.

He knew those eyes in an instant, and his body was flooded with a kind of gratitude and emotion that only comes from desiring something with all one's heart. Rick knew that he was looking into the eyes of a miracle. They were the same eyes he had seen in his dream, the same eyes Armando had worked so hard to capture on paper, the same eyes that he had been looking for all these weeks. There was no mistaking who she was; Armando's drawing had captured her, right down to the funny little cowlick that gave her bangs a funny part.

He sat transfixed in front of his computer, almost afraid to believe what he was seeing.

As Rick sat there, looking into those already familiar eyes, his secretary walked into his office. Jennifer began talking to him, but the words were only a dull buzz in his ears.

"Are you okay?" she asked, realizing that he hadn't taken his eyes off the computer screen since she had walked into the room. His normally booming voice was quiet as he spoke.

"I think I found her, Jennifer. Come here, look at this picture and tell me if you think it's her."

"Rick, you don't need me to tell you. You'll know in your heart …" Jennifer began.

"Just look at this and tell me what you think!"

She walked around his desk and looked at the little face on the web site.

"I know the drawing is a little bit different, but ...," he said, as if afraid he was about to be proven wrong.

Jennifer found the resemblance amazing. The hair was longer, but those eyes and her lips were unmistakably the same little girl.

"Yeah, Rick, it looks like her," Jennifer said. "I think you might have found her."

"I've got to call Stephanie," he said, picking up his phone and pounding numbers into the keypad. Rick's voice was trembling with emotion as his wife answered the phone.

"Steph, I think we've found her," he said. "You've got to get on the computer and see this."

Stephanie had never taken much interest in computers, nor had raising four children and tending to an assortment of animals given her much time to acquaint herself with cyberspace. Under normal circumstances, this didn't create any problems in their lives, but Rick could feel the anticipation welling within him as he talked Stephanie through the process of logging on and pulling up the web site of the Russian baby home.

He told her which buttons to click on, and he could feel his heart pounding inside his chest as he waited for her to experience what he already had been through.

"Oh good heavens!" she gasped. Stephanie was filled with awe and amazement as the little child's face peered back at her from the computer screen. "I know that face!"

The couple sat in front of their respective computers, forty-five minutes away from one another, and looked at the child they had been waiting for God to deliver.

"She looks like Maria," Stephanie said, marveling at how closely the child resembled their oldest daughter at that age. Their features were almost identical; it was as if they had been born from the same parents.

Rick was ready to get on a plane at that moment, wanted to leave then and there to go pick up his daughter. He dialed the now-familiar phone number to The Open Door Adoption Agency; each ring seemed to take forever as Rick waited for someone to pick up the phone. As soon as he heard Ed Thomas' voice on the other end, the emotion erupted through the phone.

"We found her," he said.

"Oh my gosh. Are you serious?" Ed asked, scrambling to call up the site. They had spoken to one another less than ten minutes earlier, when Rick had called Ed to inform him that they had received the final piece of paperwork to make them eligible to adopt a child overseas.

Just as Rick had done moments earlier, Ed watched as the information and picture loaded onto his computer screen. It was, unmistakably, the little child from the drawing Rick had sent him. Ed felt himself filled with a sense of awe; he had never doubted the child's existence, had never bothered questioning whether or not they would find her. But to see those eyes looking back at him filled him with a humbling and powerful reminder of God's presence.

The buzz took mere seconds to circulate around his nine-person office, and within moments the entire staff was huddled around his computer, looking at the photo that matched the drawing upon Ed's desk. Years of working with adoptive families had given the staff a familiarity with the joy of placing a child in a loving home, but nothing had prepared them for the emotions that filled the room at this moment. She was, without a doubt, the child they had been looking for; there wasn't a single dry eye in the room.

"What do we do now?" Rick asked.

Ed told Rick that he would contact Russia immediately and begin the process; he would call Rick back later in the day once he had more information. Rick hung up the phone and then promptly began dialing again.

Vince was driving down Plant Street in Winter Garden when his cell phone rang.

"We found her. Vince, I think we found her," Rick's voice burst across the line. He paused, correcting himself and omitting the hesitancy of the word "think."

"No, we found her. We have her picture."

Vince was momentarily breathless, completely overwhelmed by what he had just heard.

"What? Are you kidding me? You found her?"

"Yes! I'm sitting here looking at her right now!" Vince shook his head in amazement.

"I'm ten minutes away," he said. "I'll be right there."

Rick copied the photo from the website and began printing it out. He emailed it to his sister, Dianne, and waited for Vince to arrive. Vince rushed in, winded with anticipation. The rest of the office was huddled around Rick's desk, where Rick sat cradling his laptop. Vince stepped in behind his brother and was amazed by what he saw.

The details of Armando's drawing were replicated on the computer screen; Vince was astounded at how tiny, simple elements now seemed so important. Like everyone else who saw the picture that day, Vince was drawn to the funny little part in her bangs and the unique pout of her lips. But it was her eyes that said the most.

They were enormous and sad, as sad as the child in the drawing and as sad as the little girl Rick had hugged close to him while he slept in the wee hours of the morning just three weeks earlier. Her eyes begged for someone to hold her, love her, to let her know that everything would be okay.

Vince had never doubted his brother's mission, but he also had not expected events to move so quickly. He was in shock as he looked at the little face and he asked his older brother what the next step was.

"We have to wait to hear back from Ed Thomas," Rick explained. "He's working to find out more about her and what we need to do."

Vince could see that his brother was more determined than ever before. His concern had shifted from the mission to find the little girl into a concern about how to get her home. Rick finished printing out copies of the picture and rushed out the door. It was about noon, and he knew he could find his parents at home.

"Where are you going?" Vince asked.

"Mom and Dad's. I'll be on my cell phone."

Rick could hardly contain himself as he climbed into his car. He called Joe Lyons, who was working at his office in Universal Studios that day.

"Joe, you're not going to believe this," he said.

Joe was immediately caught off guard by Rick's voice; it sounded as if he could hardly breathe.

"Rick, are you okay? What? What is it?"

"Oh my gosh, Joe. We found her. I can't believe it! We found her Joe!"

Joe felt his jaw dropping. It was one thing to believe something would occur; it was quite another to witness it unfolding.

"What? Where?"

Rick offered what few details he knew; that the little girl was two and a half years old and was living in a baby home in Russia. Beyond that, all Rick knew was that he was ready to bring her home.

The conversation was brief, leaving Joe with more questions than answers. Rick was eager to get off the phone, eager to get on to his next call. He promised to email Joe the little girl's picture later that day, and Joe found himself keeping a close eye on his email, anticipating the arrival of the photo.

Joe knew that there was absolutely no way that Rick should have been able to find that little girl. The cop that remained inside of him, more than a decade after he had retired from the profession, told him that there was no way this should have occurred. And even though the believer in him had never doubted that Rick would find her, Joe, like Vince, also was astonished that the events had happened so quickly.

Richard and Carmelita were eating when their oldest child appeared, unannounced, on their doorstep. It was out of the ordinary for Rick to show up without calling first, and Carmelita's heart immediately began racing, fearing something was wrong. It was obvious that Rick had been crying as he entered, and she braced herself for the worst.

"What is it? Is someone sick?" she asked, her maternal concern overriding reason and encouraging her mind to race to the worst-case scenarios.

"No," Rick replied, shaking his head. "Nothing's wrong. We found her."

He held out the photo he had printed from the web site, and Carmelita released an audible gasp.

"Here she is," Rick said, tenderly handing the little girl's picture over to his parents.

Carmelita was immediately drawn to the little girl's eyes. She could not recall ever seeing such sadness, and she could not imagine what might have made such a young, innocent child feel so sad.

"She looks like a little baby doll..." Carmelita said, her voice trailing off as they looked at the photo. "She's beautiful. She looks just like Maria!"

Rick nodded and answered, to the best of his ability, many of the same questions that still lurked in his mind. He only knew that she was in Russia; until he heard from Ed, he wouldn't know how they were to proceed or how long the process might take. Rick only knew that, at last, the little girl from his dream had a name.

Nadezchda, he would learn later that day, translates into the Americanized name Nadia – meaning "hope." It seemed to Rick like just one more piece falling into place in a spiritual puzzle.

He waited impatiently for Ed to return his call; Rick had expected to hear from him within moments, but as the afternoon stretched on and he still had heard nothing, Rick found the waiting unbearable. He called the adoption agency, but was unable to reach Ed, and turned his attention back to emailing Nadia's photo to friends. When Ed's phone number finally appeared on his Caller ID, he found himself heaving a huge sigh of relief.

The good news, Ed told him, was that the child on the web site was living in the orphanage in Pechory, in the region of Pskov. The home was about a twelve-hour train ride from Moscow, then it would take one more hour in a car to actually reach the baby home, which was near the Estonian border.

Rick was filled with questions, and they tumbled out randomly. When could they go get her? Was she alright? What did they know about her?

Ed explained that his agency had a representative in Pskov, and that they would send someone to the orphanage to check on Nadia and evaluate her health. They would provide Rick with a full report on her as soon as they could, but, he cautioned, it wasn't as simple as jumping on a plane and going to Russia. While they were certain that they had found the little girl Rick first had found in his dream, Ed had discovered that she was not available for international adoption at this time.

Rick refused to believe what he was hearing. How could his baby not be ready to come home to live with him? He had seen her picture, had seen those precious eyes looking back at him, beckoning him to hold her, just as he had done in that dark basement. Rick had come this far by faith; he knew there had to be an answer.

Ed explained that when a child is placed in a Russian orphanage, they are placed on a database for three months, giving any other family members the chance to claim her. Since Nadia had only been in the orphanage for a few weeks, she wasn't yet up for adoption. According to policy, she would be available for domestic adoption after three months, and then, after six months of living in the orphanage, she would be available for international adoption.

Rick counted off the months on the calendar; that meant Nadia would not even be ready for adoption until June. He couldn't fathom waiting that long. It already seemed as if the weeks since he had first started looking for her had dragged on for months; it was hard for him to remember a time when his thoughts weren't consumed with this precious little girl. But there was more.

Rick and Stephanie's home had only been approved for international adoption that very day; that meant that their paperwork had not yet been submitted to Russia. Fortunately, Ed explained, they could submit Rick and Stephanie's paperwork to a specific region and say that they preferred to adopt from that area. The only danger was that another couple or family might already be waiting for a child from that same area. And, since the paperwork was processed on a first-come, first-served basis, if another couple was waiting in line for a child of that age from that region, it was possible they would adopt Nadia first.

Ed had seen plenty of problems arise as two families would end up fighting for the same child. Russia's limited technology meant paperwork was done by hand, which slowed the cross-referencing process. Because of such problems, the country had enacted a system that requires prospective parents to make two trips to Russia before the adoption is finalized. They also no longer allowed families to "select" a child. A representative from the orphanage would provide adopting families with basic medical information, but were no longer allowed to pass along specific information and pictures of the child.

Once a couple's paperwork was approved and a child had been matched to their request, the parents would then travel to Russia and meet their prospective child for the first time. At that point, they would complete the paperwork requesting to adopt that specific child, then would return to their home and wait while the paperwork was processed.

That procedure alone could take months, and Ed knew from experience that it was the most difficult part of the process. Once the Russian government had processed its paperwork, the new parents would be invited back to finalize the adoption and then could return home with their child.

It seemed like an eternal process; Rick could not imagine having to wait that long. He expressed his concern to Ed.

"I know, I know," Ed said, fully feeling the intensity of Rick's angst. "But this is the only way we can do it. We just have to turn it all over to God and have faith that you're going to get that child."

They submitted the paperwork to the Russian government, requesting adoption of a female, under the age of four, in the region of Pskov, for Rick and Stephanie Silanskas. Ed worked directly with Katarina, a facilitator in Pskov, and made her aware of the situation. Although there was nothing they could do officially, he would be able to at least keep an eye on Nadia through Katarina and keep Rick updated of any changes in her status.

From the outside, it appeared as if there was nothing for Rick and Stephanie to do but wait. Yet waiting was one thing that Rick didn't do well; he simply could not remain idle even under normal circumstances and now, with his little girl in an orphanage just thirty hours away by plane, train and automobile, he became a whirl of activity.

There were plenty of details to tend to, such as driving to Miami to get visas for Stephanie and him and making sure their passports were in order. It was both a torturous and joyous time for the couple, with the days seeming as if they dragged on forever, even as the couple prepared for their new daughter. When that phone call came, they wanted to be ready, and once all the paperwork was in place, Rick looked at the phone expectantly, as if thinking it should ring simply because he was waiting.

Rick continued to tell others about his miraculous dream and its subsequent discovery. Nadia's photo from the orphanage website became the screensaver on his computer, and he spent hours just watching the little face he knew so well but was unable to bring home.

Shortly after he had told his family about the pre-Christmas dream, Rick had called his old friend Jimmy Huckaby, asking Jimmy to meet him for lunch. Like so many of his colleagues who turned into dear friends, Rick and Jimmy had first met while working on a film project. Jimmy, a freelance director and producer, had directed numerous television specials, including the Disney Christmas parades and segments for the contemporary Mickey Mouse Club programs. Rick knew him to be a gentle-spirited man, one who was humble but competent and always made Rick feel at ease.

The two met at the Millennia Mall, where Rick told Jimmy the story of his dream and outlined his search for the little girl. At the time, Jimmy's response had been similar to Joe Lyons' reaction.

"You've got to get this on film," he encouraged Rick. "You have to document this so people will believe it."

At the time, Rick was far too preoccupied with the mission directly before him to be concerned with the filming process. As the men met for lunch again later that month, Rick was thrilled to be able to reveal to Jimmy that he had found the little girl in the dream. As he told the story about the web site, and of finding Nadia just moments after he learned they had been approved for international adoption, Jimmy felt the Goosebumps on his arms.

He was excited and wanted to help Rick tell the story. By now, Rick had had enough time to become comfortable with the notion of putting his story on tape, and he gave Jimmy his blessing to embark on the project. Rick gave Jimmy a list of people to contact about the events that were happening, knowing that Jimmy would take the project and run with it.

It seemed as if the flurry of activity came from every direction. Jimmy began to contact the key people in Rick's life, arranging interviews and taping them for what would later become an award-winning documentary. Meanwhile, Rick's focus turned entirely to what was happening in Russia, and he felt that he was both racing against time and urging it to hurry up and pass more quickly.

The creation of The Project Anna Foundation had given a new reason for DreamVision to thrive, and throughout February and March, Vince and Rick worked diligently to build a strong base for the non-profit organization. The seed that had been planted in Rick's head was now blossoming into a fruitful endeavor as Rick dreamed of opening doors that barred many families from adopting a child who desperately longed for their love.

"Money should never be the only thing that keeps a loving family from adopting a child," he explained to Vince. "We can create a way to help parents who want a child."

Rick had found the statistics in Russia nothing short of staggering. Of the nearly one million children living in Russia's orphanages, about ninety-five percent of them still have a living parent. And because so many birth parents fail to sign over their rights, more than half of the children who are orphaned or abandoned never make it onto the country's database, which means they will never be eligible for adoption. Only about one-fourth of the country's orphans are available for international adoption, and after a child reaches school age, his or her chance of being adopted is less than five percent.

After that, their futures begin looking even more grim: Roughly half the girls raised in orphanages are forced into prostitution after leaving the home; nearly half of all orphans become homeless and about ten percent of them commit suicide.

The numbers brought tears to Rick's eyes. He couldn't imagine how so many children could live their lives without loving parents, without much hope for the future. The more he learned, the more determined he became to do something about it. With The Project Anna Foundation, he believed they could make small changes that would have a big impact.

Rick's every waking thought seemed devoted to the orphans in Russia and to Nadia in particular. He was rarely seen at the DreamVision offices, remaining accessible to Vince by phone. He spent most of his energy working on developing the non-profit organization. Keeping busy, it seemed, was the only way to stave off the incredible sadness that had filled him when he learned that it would be months before he would be able to hold Nadia in his arms, and it would take even longer for him to be able to bring her home.

He prayed fervently and non-stop, asking God to move swiftly, to tear down the walls and expedite the paperwork that stood between his family and the Russian government. Rick stayed in constant contact with Ed Thomas, checking in at least once a week to see if anything had changed. Despite his resolve to move forward, Rick found that there were days when the emptiness overwhelmed him, when talking to people seemed just too great a challenge. It was then that he would disappear, driving to a secluded park overlooking a lake, where he would spend hours talking to God.

At that point in time, it was as if God was the only one who could possibly begin understanding how Rick felt. Nothing would fill the hole carved into his heart by Nadia's absence, and his life, once so full, now seemed incomplete.

On those days when he needed to sequester himself from the rest of the world, Rick would turn off his cell phone and disappear.

Nobody knew where he went or when he would return; Vince would find himself in the position of fielding phone calls from clients or colleagues, assuring them that everything was fine and that projects would be delivered on time. Then Vince would track down Rick, oftentimes having to go through Stephanie, who was equally uninformed as to where Rick might be hiding that day.

Stephanie had been Rick's rock and voice of reason from the day they married. Now, it was up to her to intervene and pull him back into the present. Understanding that her husband was aching for the little girl in the Russian orphanage, she would also remind him that he had a family and life here in Florida that needed his attention. Each time he submerged himself in his thoughts and prayer, he would return from the experience rejuvenated and more determined than ever to get that little girl home safely. His concern was no longer just for her; he was haunted by what he had learned about the lives of orphans, and was convinced that he must do something about it.

Everywhere he went, whether it was work-related or social, Rick felt compelled to share his story. Business meetings were thrown entirely off track as Rick would interrupt the intended order of business to instead tell his story. Anybody who encountered him during that time would hear about the little girl in the dream that he now knew was waiting for him in an orphanage on the other side of the world.

Reaction to Rick's story was mixed; most people felt stirred by what they often viewed as an amazing string of coincidences, others immediately declared it an amazing act of God. Some took a more skeptical posturing, listening politely to Rick's story but adopting a more cynical attitude, choosing not to fully believe the story until they had actually seen the little girl in the flesh.

Their responses made no difference in Rick's determination to spread his story; he knew what he had seen and felt, and he was adamant that everyone who came in touch with him would know about it.

DreamVision continued pursuing an animated film version telling the story of Rick and Nadia, and in February they began meeting with anyone and everyone who would listen to their story. With Joe Lyons now on board full-time, they were able to utilize Joe's contacts in the movie industry and had daily business meetings with prospective investors; they traveled to Los Angeles to meet with casting agents and movie executives, hoping to get the project off the ground.

The City of Angels is where movie magic comes to life, but it also is a cold, hard machine that devours thousands of dreams every day. In Los Angeles, Rick and Vince found a tepid reception; they were told it was a nice story, but asked not to talk so much about God. It just was not *done* that way in Hollywood, they were told. And besides, as nice as their story was – it still lacked a powerful ending.

Nobody knew that any better than Rick. The ending to his story, the fulfillment of his miracle, was all that was on his heart. He returned from Los Angeles more determined than ever to tell his story, but also more devastated than ever as the wait for Nadia continued dragging on.

The months of waiting through Stephanie's pregnancies seemed like nothing compared to the open-ended waiting they were enduring now. At least as an expectant father he had been able to take action; he could see evidence of the child growing within his wife, could paint rooms and prepare nurseries for the impending arrival. In this case, he had nothing but a photo to cling to, nothing but faith to keep him motivated from one day to the next.

He would alternately submerge and then resurface, oftentimes requiring prompting from either Vince or Stephanie to come back to the challenges and situations at hand. At times, Vince found himself having to be very specific with Rick, outlining exactly what needed to be accomplished and giving him a structured time frame in which to get it done. At other times, Rick would emerge from his spiritual hibernation as a man on fire, again invigorated and bent on completing each and every task that needed his attention.

The calendar slowly moved forward and the days grew longer. Rick and Stephanie hoped that spring would bring their new daughter home. His days already seemed to last forever, and extended hours of daylight only seemed to keep him farther away from the next morning, which he prayed would begin with the phone call they were waiting for. Stephanie was growing concerned over Rick's behavior. Three months after finding Nadia's photo, they had very little new information to go on. They had learned that the baby home which housed Nadia was a medical orphanage, not a social facility, but they were given only bare-bones details as to her status. They knew that she was considered developmentally delayed and that she barely spoke, but had little information beyond that. Each day Rick and Stephanie entrusted their daughter to God's care, prayed for her continued health and well-being and prayed that this would be the day they were called to come meet her.

Easter Sunday fell on April 20 that year, and the entire Silanskas clan gathered at Dianne's home to celebrate it. Talk centered around Nadia, as it always did these days, and Dianne was concerned for her older brother. He was driven and determined, but she could see the panic he felt over needing to have his daughter living under his roof. Stephanie was eager but pragmatic, wanting to have events happen quickly but also knowing that it all would unfold in God's time. Dianne continued to be amazed and impressed by Stephanie, who had so willingly abandoned her plans to embrace Rick's vision. The dreams of an easier time, of a more leisurely life, would vanish with the addition of a young child, and Dianne listened as Stephanie explained how God had prepared her heart for this moment, had made her ready to accept this huge step in a surprising new direction.

It broke Carmelita's heart to see her son struggling with his ordeal. The stress of waiting for the phone to ring was etched in Rick's face, and despite his determination, he also looked somewhat worn from his constant vigil. Carmelita had surprised the entire family by her warm reception to Rick's news, but no one was more surprised by it than Carmelita herself. Although she had long expressed concerns about her ability to accept an adopted child as family, she had made an amazing transformation, now wholeheartedly looking forward to the day she could welcome her new granddaughter home.

Carmelita had already become Nadia's biggest fan, and seemed as eager as Rick himself to get her arms around that precious little child.

Easter's promise of rebirth came to fruition just hours later. Rick was in his car when Ed's phone call came the following morning.

"They're ready for you to come meet your daughter," Ed informed him, his smile traveling over the phone line.

Rick nearly dropped the phone. Months of anxiety washed out of his body as his eyes filled with tears that spilled down his cheeks. Rick felt swept away by the enormous wave of relief that flooded his heart and soul.

"Thank you God. Thank you!"

Rick could not find any other words. The magnitude of his gratitude was beyond anything he could describe or comprehend. He had lived for this moment for the past four months, and to finally have it in sight filled him with emotions that left him awed by their enormity.

"When? What do we do?" Rick began, getting the details he needed before calling Stephanie. Ed walked through the process with him, outlining what needed to occur. Rick and Stephanie would be in Russia the following week, which was the last week of April. After months of waiting, they were only days away from holding little Nadia in their arms.

"But Rick, you've got to remember," Ed cautioned. "You can't bring her home. You have to leave her there."

Rick could not imagine being reunited with that precious little girl from his dreams, only to have to leave her behind. He refused to accept that as acceptable or even possible.

"We've got to do everything we can to change that, Ed," he said, as determined as he had been about finding her in the first place. "I can't leave her there. We've got to find a way to bring her back with us."

Ed knew that Russian law would not allow that to occur, but Rick was convinced that it was possible. Rick knew the power of prayer and knew that God would continue working His miracles. He already had led Rick and Stephanie right to this little girl – how could He deny them the right to bring her home? Rick called Stephanie as soon as he got off the phone with Ed.

"Ed just called me," he said unable to contain the excitement in his voice. "They're ready for us to go to Russia! Let's go get our baby."

Chapter Ten

The days following Easter couldn't fly by fast enough as Rick and Stephanie made final preparations for their trip to Russia. The experience was reminiscent of the last few days of a pregnancy; after months of anticipation and preparation, the suitcase was packed and now their minds were filled with last-minute questions and what-ifs.

It was a scenario that Ed Thomas had experienced numerous times, and he wasn't surprised by the number of phone calls he received from Rick as the days ticked down. All of the anxiety of prospective adoptive parents seems to peak right before they make their journey, and Rick and Stephanie were no exception.

Ed knew from experience that the hardest part of this trip would not be the grueling travel schedule, but rather would come from having to leave the little child behind in the orphanage. According to Russian regulations, the prospective adoptive parents could only visit the child for one hour per day for three days; they would then have to return home and wait for the paperwork to be processed and approval to be granted. Ed tried preparing Rick for that separation, but Rick remained determined not to suffer that fate.

"We have to do everything we can so that doesn't happen," he told Ed adamantly. "I can't leave my baby there. I want to bring her home with us."

Ed assured Rick that he would be on call to do whatever he could and to provide whatever support Rick needed while he and Stephanie were abroad.

They made arrangements for their week-long absence. With Tony living at home again, he could keep an eye on Jessica and Andrew as well as watching over the family's assortment of animals. The children all walked out to the car as they loaded the suitcases into the trunk; the family stood there in a rare moment of silence as the reality sank in. It wasn't as if their lives were about to change; their lives already had been permanently changed by the child who, up until now, only Rick had seen. But everyone in the family had been living with her in one way or another for the past four months, and they all were anxious for their parents to go meet their new sister and bring back photos and news about her. They prayed together for a safe trip before Tony drove his parents to the Orlando International Airport. He felt a tremendous sense of pride as he deposited them at the gate.

Tony had never met anybody who had the kind of unwavering faith he had seen in his father. At an age where most young men are trying to distance themselves from their families, Tony wanted to bask in his. He found Rick's faith inspiring, found himself challenged to live a better life just by watching the way his father operated in the world. He had trusted his father his entire life, and from the time Rick had told them about the dream of the little girl, he had believed that she existed and that he would find her.

He had seen Rick embark on numerous adventures during the course of his life, some with better results than others. This time, though, it had been different. Rick didn't pause to think this through, he didn't take time to sit down and logically consider a more reasonable explanation to his dream. Instead, he had jumped in with both feet, a leap of faith from which he could not be deterred. Although Tony was excited for what this meant for the entire family, he was most touched and inspired by his father's ability to listen to the still, small voice of God as it spoke to him through the big brown eyes of a tiny child.

Rick and Stephanie faced a demanding travel schedule; after a quick flight up the coast to New York, they would take a sixteen-hour flight to Moscow, where they would spend the night. The following afternoon they would board a train for the twelve-hour ride to Pechory, and from there they would take another hour-long car ride to the orphanage where Nadia was living. It left Rick and Stephanie with plenty of time to think about what lay ahead and to wonder out loud what it would be like to be joined – or, in Rick's case, reunited – with the little girl from his dream.

As they arrived in Moscow the next morning, it felt as if they were stepping out of their own lives and entering a movie set that rivaled "Dr. Zhivago." A cold wind whipped around them, blowing snow through the air. The scene was magical and it reminded them just how far away they were from the comforts of their Florida home. They were met at the airport by Alex, a liaison provided by The Open Door Adoption Agency to escort them throughout Moscow and serve as a translator. Alex was a charming young man and a delightful guide; he was polite and accommodating, eager to make Rick and Stephanie as comfortable as possible. He took them to their hotel, where the couple took a nap before going out to explore the city on their own.

"We need to hear some music," Stephanie suggested as they mulled over their options. Music was such a powerful, healing force in their lives, and it seemed that the calming influence would benefit both of them.

At the New Bolshoi Theater, they were able to see the Moscow Symphony Orchestra perform as part of an Easter celebration. The powerful and emotional performance of the renowned symphony only added to the surreal feeling of the night. Neither Rick nor Stephanie had ever thought about traveling to Russia, let alone going there to open a new chapter in their lives. As they stood on the other side of the world, completely alone together, they felt anticipation and anxiety colliding and subsiding. It was both exhilarating and exhausting as they prepared to take the next step of their journey.

Alex joined them the next day, accompanying them to Moscow's famous Red Square before taking them to the train station. Rick felt as if he were in a dream as they stood in front of the famous St. Basil's Cathedral, transfixed by the swirling, colorful towers that compose the magnificent building.

"I can't believe we're here," he said to Stephanie as they gazed at their surroundings. She looked at him, equally amazed by the experience. As their eyes met, Rick felt a warmth sweep over him. He was so grateful for God's goodness in his life, so grateful to have a woman like Stephanie as his wife to stand beside him. At that moment, they both knew they were where God wanted them to be, and the feeling that cascaded over them seemed to shield them from the sharp Moscow air.

Alex accompanied them to the Leningratsky Station, where they were scheduled for a seven o'clock departure. The trip would last through the night, and it seemed unbelievable to Rick that he and Stephanie would be reunited with Nadia the very next day. He was excited but nervous, as if he was seeing a family member that he had not seen in a very long time.

They were silent for most of the trip, alternately sleeping and looking out the window at the Russian countryside as they sped through it. Rick was particularly quiet and they were grateful for the privacy of their compartment, which allowed them to be alone together. As Stephanie slept, Rick prayed and watched the world that he had just discovered slip away. Moscow's majestic buildings had given way to tiny villages that dotted the landscape, and the train stations became increasingly more dilapidated. He felt as if he were in a movie, thrust into a role he could never have imagined in a world he never even knew existed. Rick was fascinated with what he saw, and as the cloak of night surrendered to the first rays of morning light, he watched as farmers tended to their livestock, oblivious to the train cutting through the otherwise bucolic setting.

It was just after seven a.m. when the train pulled into the station. Before Rick and Stephanie had the chance to gather their things and leave the train, two women entered their compartment.

Ludmilla, the translator, explained that they were there to accompany Rick and Stephanie on the rest of their journey. The other woman was Katarina, the facilitator who had worked with Nadia's orphanage.

They were kind and gracious women, eager to help Rick and Stephanie in every way they could. Despite Rick's insistence to let him and Stephanie carry their own luggage, the two women took their bags and helped carry the suitcases from the train to the waiting car. It was a tiny European compact model, and they were barely able to fit the luggage and four adults inside.

The first stop for Rick and Stephanie was their hotel. Ludmilla explained that the couple would have about fifteen minutes to get refreshed and prepare for the rest of their day. After that, they were to visit the regional Kremlin and have an audience with the minister of education, who needed to see them before they continued on to the orphanage.

Rick and Stephanie exchanged a puzzled glance; Ed had not told them they needed to visit with the minister of education.

"Why? Is there a problem?" Rick asked, feeling somewhere between uncomfortable and alarmed.

Ludmilla shook her head and reiterated that the minister of education simply wanted to meet with them. It was a common practice for the Department of Education to meet with families that are considering adoption; while primarily a formality, the policy allows officials to ensure that the prospective family has the best interest of the child in mind.

After depositing their bags at the hotel, Rick and Stephanie joined Katarina and Ludmilla in the tiny car. Rick and Stephanie nervously entered the Kremlin with their Russian guides, and were directed to the Department of Education. Feeling a bit like Dorothy cautiously entering the kingdom of Oz, they entered and sat quietly, waiting to be addressed. The minister of education was a stern-looking woman in her fifties, and she continued writing on a piece of paper as the guests sat quietly and waited patiently to see what was about to happen. Behind her sat a video monitor; Nadia's picture was on the screen.

Rick's heart and head were racing as he wondered what it all meant. Finally, after a few moments that hung in the air like an eternity, the minister of education put down her pencil. She looked up and addressed Rick and Stephanie in flawless English.

"Mr. and Mrs. Silanskas," she began, studying the American couple carefully. "I am familiar with your case. I know of your dream and of how you came to find Nadezchda."

She cleared her throat, moved by the story she had heard, then continued.

"Mr. and Mrs. Silanskas, this is a miracle of God. I impatiently wait your return after you have been to the orphanage to meet your daughter."

They left the Department of Education feeling empowered by the visit. They had known all along that this was a miracle, but to hear it declared as such in the Kremlin left them speechless.

The ride to the orphanage took them across winding country roads to the small town of Pechory. They had been in the car for nearly an hour when they came upon the Pechory Monastery, a picturesque sixteenth-century monastery that remains active today. Rick and Stephanie were awed by the impressive fortress, and they continued to gaze at the sprawling campus as the car turned a corner onto a narrow dirt road. Just half a mile down the dirt road stood an old building, worn from years of fighting the harsh weather and even harder times. The car pulled up and Rick caught his breath, unable to believe that they were finally there.

As they looked up at the aging building with grimy windows, a bit of movement in one of the upstairs windows caught their eyes. The curtains had been pulled away, and a tiny pair of hands pressed up against the window. Just beyond those hands was a tiny face looking down at the car.

The sight was a touching one, and Rick reached for Stephanie's hand as they exchanged a sorrowful look.

"They do that every day," Ludmilla explained, noticing the couple's reaction.

"They're hoping that the next car that comes will be a car to take them home."

Her words shot through Rick and Stephanie's hearts, resonating with a lasting chill. They realized that, as prepared as they thought they were, there was truly nothing that could fully fortify them for what they were about to experience.

"My legs feel like jelly," he whispered to Stephanie as they got out of the car. "I don't know if I can walk up those stairs!"

Months of prayer and anticipation were melting away, leaving him emotionally charged for the moments that lay before them. He took Stephanie's hand and they followed Ludmilla and Katarina. As they were about to mount the stairs, Ludmilla turned and reminded them that this was a medical orphanage, not a social orphanage.

"She is severely developmentally delayed," Ludmilla said, cautioning them for what they were about to experience. "She doesn't speak much, and if she runs from you, don't be alarmed. These children are only used to seeing women. All the workers here are women. They're often afraid of men."

It was a warning Rick and Stephanie already had heard, but Rick refused to pay it heed.

"She'll know," he had assured Stephanie. "She'll be fine. I *know* this child."

They entered the orphanage and were escorted to a waiting area. Sitting on an old floral couch, it seemed as if mere seconds had passed before a worker entered the room. She held Nadia's little hands in hers, directing her into the room and turning her in Rick and Stephanie's direction. Stephanie gasped.

"Oh my goodness! Look how small she is!"

She was just as tiny as she had been in the dream. She wore a dark jumper over a red turtleneck, and her head sported a huge white bow. The huge brown eyes that had haunted Rick for months looked directly at him, hesitating for a moment. The worker gave Nadia a slight nudge, and Rick held his hands out toward her.

On unsteady legs, the child held her tiny hands out and wobbled over to where Rick was sitting. He took her tiny hands in his own, finally physically touching the precious child his arms had ached to embrace. Nadia gazed up at him, then looked to his left, where

Stephanie sat beside Rick. One little hand reached out to Stephanie, and as Stephanie extended her arms, Nadia ran into them.

The orphanage workers watched in amazement as the scene played out. Rick felt a huge wave of relief and thanksgiving wash over him; it was as if they had always been together. Stephanie pulled Nadia up into her lap and the child looked up at her with a smile. Rick reached out and picked up the soft stuffed toy puppy they had brought her. He held it out toward her and Nadia eagerly grabbed it, hugging it close to her chest.

Rick took his daughter in his arms and she sank into his chest, letting Rick embrace her. She held tight to her new toy, and Rick gently rocked her back and forth.

"She's beautiful," he whispered to Stephanie, his voice choked with emotion. Stephanie smiled, taken in by the child's beauty. The resemblance to Maria, their oldest daughter, was uncanny and Stephanie already felt as if she had known this child forever.

Nadia was fighting a severe respiratory infection, and limited access to medical supplies put the orphanage workers at a disadvantage to treat her condition. As Nadia rested her head on Stephanie's shoulder, Stephanie rocked her back and forth, and she could hear the labored breathing from the small child.

"We've got to do something for her," Rick said. Stephanie nodded. This child was already intricately intertwined with them, and all they wanted to do at this moment was to take away any pain and suffering she might feel.

"Why don't you play the piano?" Stephanie suggested, nodding toward the old upright sitting in the orphanage.

Rick's prowess on the piano was something he had used to entertain his own children, as well as his niece and nephews, for years. With no other activities available in the orphanage, and with Nadia not feeling well, Stephanie thought it might be a nice way to bring a smile to the little girl's face.

Rick sat at the piano and began running his fingers over the keys. It was a far cry from the Bosendorfer grand pianos he was accustomed to playing, but the music filled the orphanage like a symphony. Nadia's eyes lit up as she watched him play. He looked at her as she watched him from Stephanie's arms and he could see the life they had before them. Rick couldn't wait to sit with her in his own home, playing music for this beautiful little girl.

The couple took turns holding their long-lost child, and time, which had dragged its feet so slowly for so many months, now seemed to run at warp speed. The allotted hour was done all too quickly. As the orphanage workers approached Rick to take Nadia from his arms, the joy that had filled his heart for the past hour seemed to vanish. His eyes filled with tears as he and Stephanie watched the orphanage worker carry her away. Nadia's big eyes stared back at them over the worker's shoulder as she was carried through the swinging double doors that led back to the common area.

Stephanie stared tearfully at Rick, who drew his wife into his arms. She rested her head on his shoulder.

"We have to take her back home with us," Rick said. "I can't leave her here. I can't do it, Steph."

She nodded, knowing that her husband's faith and determination had brought them this far, so anything was possible.

Rick and Stephanie had been shaken by what they had seen at the orphanage; although the workers did their best to make the children comfortable, there were too many children living in too small a space. The aging building was a far cry from accommodations in the United States. The shower was nothing more than a sink with cold running water. Rick's heart went out to each of the children who called this place home because he knew he could not just turn his head and leave with little Nadia. Every face he had seen was now part of his memory forever.

"Can you take us to some of the other orphanages?" he asked Ludmilla. She nodded as Rick and Stephanie's education into the challenging world of underprivileged Russian children began. They were stunned by what they saw; they were even more shocked by the statistics. Children with disabilities didn't have access to physical therapy or aids that would help keep them mobile, so they often were left lying down most of the time. The orphanages themselves tended to be old and badly in need of repair, without central heat or air conditioning. Some lacked running water, so the children drew their water from a well each day.

Food was often scarce. Many children suffered from malnutrition because of the diet of bread, soup and water that barely sustained them. Fruits and vegetables were a luxury beyond the children's comprehension, and even fruit juice was a rare and precious commodity.

It was a stark contrast to the life he and Stephanie enjoyed, and it tugged at his heart. He knew that they could not simply leave with Nadia; he now saw a much bigger picture emerging. But for the moment, his primary concern was getting Nadia back in good health and taking her home with them.

"Ludmilla, we have to take her back with us," Rick pleaded. "Tell me what we need to do. We'll do anything, anything at all – just tell us. We'll go talk to whoever we need to see. It doesn't matter – we just can't leave her here."

Ludmilla listened, sympathetically, having seen many distraught adoptive parents through her years as a translator. She knew that there was likely nothing that could be done, but she promised Rick and Stephanie that she would do everything she could.

In their hotel that night, the minutes seemed to drag on like hours. Stephanie and Rick both were adamant about needing to return home with Nadia. They mostly stayed in their room, leaving only to visit a drug store and buy some medicine to help ease little Nadia's respiratory infection. As Rick and Stephanie returned to their hotel, they noticed a little park filled with children playing with their parents. The well-worn clothing reflected the economic challenges facing the general Russian population, and Rick and Stephanie watched as the families, oblivious for the moment to their physical lack, reveled in the greatest gift a parent can receive – a child's love.

Rick would have gladly traded every one of his creature comforts simply to trade places with them, to be the parent happily playing with a laughing Nadia in a small Russian park. Nothing in his life had ever meant so much to him. It was at that moment he knew that his material possessions would never again amount to much worth in his life.

That night they called family members, checking in and telling the story of meeting Nadia in person for the first time. Each time he told the story, he reiterated his need to bring her home with them.

"I can't leave her here. I just can't do it," he repeated time after time. "We have to find a way to bring her home with us."

As he relayed those words to Ed Thomas, Ed cautioned Rick, reminding him that this was out of their control.

Ed knew, from experience, that the most difficult part of the Russian adoption process came when adoptive parents had to leave their child behind and await government approval. He had seen the distress created from that separation, but had never seen anyone as determined as Rick to keep that from happening. Ed believed that Rick felt the pain of separation more profoundly because he felt that he had already known Nadia for so long. As a father of two young sons, Ed could put himself in Rick's shoes and imagine the lengths to which Rick would go to bring her home.

"You have to be careful, Rick. We don't make the rules," he warned. "You and I can't get in the middle of this; we have to follow their rules."

Rick listened and promised Ed he wouldn't do anything that would jeopardize the adoption process. At the same time, however, both men knew that it was impossible for Rick to sit by and do nothing.

Ludmilla and Katarina returned the next day to pick up Rick and Stephanie and return to the orphanage with them. As they made the hour-long drive, Ludmilla explained that she had looked into how they could arrange to return to the U.S. with Nadia, but the judge who handles all adoption cases was on vacation.

"We can stay longer," Rick said, desperate to make this work. "We will do whatever it takes."

Ludmilla explained that, even if they waited, the cases are arranged many months in advance. It would likely be June or July before she would have an opening to hear their case.

Rick refused to accept her words. He was not about to leave Russia without his daughter; he just had to find a way to make this work. And with God on his side, he had no doubt that he would do just that.

The orphanage workers greeted them warmly as they arrived and, moments later, a woman returned carrying Nadia. She still clutched the little stuffed puppy dog in her arms, and today she wore a bright red dress with a gigantic white lace collar that framed her face. The tiny girl perked up at the sight of her soon-to-be parents, and as Rick reached out for her she leaned into him.

The feeling of having her returned into his arms filled Rick with indescribable warmth. He hugged her close to his chest, wishing she could just melt into his heart so that he could keep her safe there.

"She doesn't look like she's feeling well," Stephanie said, hoping the medicine they brought would work quickly on her fragile system. Rick handed the child to Stephanie, who administered the medication with the stealth of a parent who had done this for many years.

Rick again sat at the piano and began to play. This time, Nadia watched from Stephanie's arms, then Rick took the little girl on his lap as he played. Her smile illuminated her entire face, filling her eyes and seeming to radiate with an intensity that seemed almost supernatural. She watched as Rick created music, and then, reluctantly, tried hitting one of the keys herself.

Rick stopped playing and hit a key, then moved his hand so Nadia could hit the same key. She happily pounded the key after him. He cheered and clapped his hands and she beamed at him. Rick began to slowly hit one note after another, and Nadia eagerly followed his every movement.

As Rick was playing, some of the orphanage workers and doctors had stepped into the room, happy to hear such beautiful music filling the room. Stephanie noticed they were talking amongst themselves, and she asked Ludmilla what they were saying.

"They don't understand," Ludmilla explained, her eyes filling with tears. "They've never seen her like this. They don't know why she's connecting with you like this."

Rick watched, stunned, as her tiny fingers followed his across the keyboard. He paused for a moment and looked at Stephanie, not believing what he was seeing. Nadia looked up at Stephanie and smiled, obviously proud of herself.

"You're very clever, aren't you?" Stephanie asked, and Nadia's smile grew even broader.

Rick and Stephanie could hardly contain the love and adoration they felt for this little child; the notion that she could have spent her life without parents to provide her loving care was simply unfathomable. As the hour-long visit abruptly came to an end, both of them were filled with grief. It felt as if they had just gotten there, yet their time was up. They knew that they had to do something; neither of them felt they had the fortitude to walk out of the orphanage the next day and leave Nadia behind.

"We have to bring her back with us," Rick told his sister on the phone that night. "Dianne, I can't leave her here. I have to get this changed. I can't come home without her."

Dianne's heart went out to her big brother; she could tell from his voice just how traumatic it was for him to leave Nadia at the orphanage overnight. Leaving Nadia at the orphanage indefinitely seemed out of the question. She promised Rick they were praying for him, and she knew that Rick truly believed God would move the mountain that stood between him and his daughter's trip to her new home in Florida.

Rick's parents were equally concerned; Carmelita was worried about the entire trip from the beginning. She felt nervous for her son, traveling to a foreign country where he and Stephanie didn't speak the language or know anyone. He had to carry money with him to pay for the adoption, and she was frightened that they would be robbed. As Rick talked to them on the phone, Carmelita and Richard's concerns moved from his physical well-being to his emotional health.

Richard could hear the distress in his son's voice, and it tore him apart. It was obvious that Rick and Stephanie were desperately in love with this child, and leaving her was the hardest thing they could imagine. Rick assured his parents that they were doing everything in their power to bring her home. And he asked them to do the only thing he knew to do – pray.

Knowing that Nadia was in need of medical care, Rick and Stephanie decided to try that avenue as a means of getting her home. They called Dr. Tafur, their longtime family doctor in Leesburg, Florida, and spent more than an hour on the phone explaining the situation. Dr. Tafur faxed a detailed letter to them outlining the medical care Nadia needed and expressing his medical opinion as to why it would behoove the child to be allowed to come home with them and receive medical treatment. The clock was ticking, and Rick and Stephanie knew it was time for another miracle to come through.

Stephanie had prepared a book full of photos of family members so that Nadia could see her new family. They had stopped at a photo processing shop on the way back from the orphanage and made prints of the pictures taken with Nadia. That night, they filled the book with pictures of her new parents and siblings so that Nadia would be able to see them even when they weren't there. The thought of leaving the little girl behind, with nothing more than a picture book and a stuffed puppy to remember them by, seemed a merciless act.

Ludmilla greeted them at their hotel the next afternoon, and she and Katarina escorted Rick and Stephanie to the orphanage for their last scheduled visit with Nadia. It seemed impossible that the drive to the orphanage took about the same amount of time as they were allowed to visit Nadia; the trip dragged on forever, while the visit took place so quickly. Rick presented Ludmilla with his paperwork from the doctor in Leesburg, but she warned him that it would take some time; she had to submit it to authorities and, even then, it might not be considered. Time was something Rick and Stephanie did not have on their side; only sixty minutes remained between them and the moment they were supposed to walk out the door without Nadia.

Rick and Stephanie felt the combination of excitement and dread as they approached the orphanage stairs. They were so happy to see Nadia again, but could not imagine leaving there without her that day.

Her smile seemed even bigger than before as the orphanage workers brought her to them. She seemed slightly better than she had been the previous day, but her breathing still was labored. Rick and Stephanie knelt down to the floor, alternately playing with her and just holding her close.

Nadia's little face looked up at Rick, studying the eyes that seemed so similar to her own. She looked at him quizzically as he put his hand over his heart and said, "Papa."

She paused for a moment, then smiled.

"Papa!" she repeated, and Rick felt the lump return to his throat. He pointed to Stephanie.

"Mama," he said.

Again, the little girl smiled.

"Mama!" she exclaimed.

Stephanie and Rick looked at each other through tear-filled eyes. Ludmilla, watching from a couch, fought to keep her composure. Rick threw his arms open wide to offer Nadia a hug. She looked at him, not sure of what to do next.

"She's never been hugged," Ludmilla explained. "She doesn't know what you want her to do."

The words nearly ripped Rick's heart from his chest as he pulled Nadia into a hug. This simple act that was so much a part of his family's daily ritual was foreign to this innocent little child. He cradled her against his chest, memorizing the way her little body fit against his own. Her tiny heart beat against him, and he felt the way he had felt when he first held each of his infants at their birth.

With the minutes ticking by far too quickly, Rick and Stephanie began to feel like a prisoner awaiting his final fate. Even as they held Nadia, they prayed for a last-minute reprieve, begged God to send them the spiritual equivalent of the governor's phone call. Instead, the double doors swung open and the orphanage worker returned.

Her eyes were soft as she motioned to Rick. He hugged Nadia closer and Stephanie joined him on the floor as thy wrapped their arms around the little child. His wet brown eyes looked into his wife's face.

"I can't do it, Stephanie. I can't let them take my baby!"

Stephanie began sobbing and Nadia looked at them, puzzled by the sudden change of emotion. Ludmilla joined them on the floor, wanting to help them but also knowing what must be done. Rick pulled Nadia closer and began crying harder; the worker reached between Rick and Stephanie and wrapped her hands around Nadia's waist.

Ludmilla patted Rick on the shoulder and he knew what his legal obligation was. He kissed his daughter, and Stephanie did the same, promising they would be back soon. They watched through their tears as Nadia disappeared through the double doors.

"I can't do this Stephanie. I can't!"

He clung tightly to his wife's hand. She could say nothing at that point as she felt the pangs of her own grief raging inside. Ludmilla spoke to them, gently, reassuring them that everything would be alright. But as they helped one another to the waiting car, Rick and Stephanie felt that nothing could be farther from the truth.

Chapter Eleven

The car ride from the orphanage back to the hotel seemed like an eternity, with both Rick and Stephanie sobbing most of the way. It seemed unimaginable that they would have to leave the country the next day without their little girl. As each mile put them farther and farther from Nadia, Rick's mind raced with ways to convince the Russian government to let him take her home with them.

Ludmilla looked at the American couple in the back seat and felt her heart going out to them. It was always difficult for prospective parents to leave a child behind, but she had rarely seen such intense displays of emotion. Everything about this story was different, and it had moved her in ways she had never experienced before. Now, as she saw the couple suffering, she wanted desperately to be able to help them.

Rick and Stephanie returned to their hotel, and Ludmilla explained that she and Katarina would return the next day and accompany them to the train station, where they would begin backtracking the route that had brought them here just four days earlier. Rick felt as if weeks, not days had passed; he felt like a different man than the one who had stepped off the train a few days earlier. Everything they had seen had made a profound, lasting impact on Rick. He knew that his purpose and mission in life would never be the same.

Back at their hotel, he and Stephanie caved in to the grief and sorrow that they had fought to contain at the orphanage. They alternately paced the room and sank onto the bed, reaching out for one another in comfort and then pulling away to try to comprehend their own individual anguish.

The afternoon had slipped into evening, and Rick left the hotel room to be alone with his thoughts. He walked the streets of Pskov for hours, finally making his way back to the park near the hotel. He watched as parents arrived with their children, and tears filled his eyes as he listened to the children's laughter. Rick pulled his cell phone from his pocket and dialed Vince's number.

Vince was having dinner with Joe Lyons at the Citrus Club, a swank restaurant overlooking Orlando, when Vince's phone rang. Rick's voice was barely audible above the conversations around Vince, but even without even being able to understand what Rick was saying, Vince could hear that his brother was heartbroken. Vince excused himself from the table to take the call outside.

Rick sat on the park bench on the other side of the world and cried out to his little brother. His distress was tangible through the telephone, and Vince longed to be able to help ease his big brother's pain.

"Vince, I don't know how to do this," Rick confessed. "I can't leave my baby here!"

They talked, brother to brother, depending upon the bond that already had seen them through so many trials together. As Rick began releasing some of the sorrow he felt, his attention expanded far beyond Nadia's plight.

"You can't believe what it's like here, Vince. It's unimaginable."

Rick told Vince of his experiences visiting the orphanages and related the dire conditions he had witnessed.

"They have nobody to help them," he said. "We've got to do something."

Vince knew at that moment that the next leg of his own journey was beginning. He didn't know where it would take them, and realized that at that moment, Rick wasn't sure, either. But Vince was absolutely convinced that the words he was hearing were setting the stage for the work they were about to take on.

As Rick spoke, he watched the parents in the park playing with their children. He described the scene for Vince.

"These people have nothing, Vince," he said. "And yet, they're here, smiling and laughing with their children. It's as if they are the happiest, richest people in the world. They find their happiness in the simple pleasures of life; there is so much we could learn from them."

The two men talked for a few more minutes and as Rick's pain temporarily subsided, they prayed together on the phone before hanging up. Vince returned to the dinner table, where their meals had arrived and Joe sat waiting for him.

Vince looked at the plate of food before him, realizing the meal he had just ordered cost several months' wages in Russia. His stomach turned at the thought.

"I can't eat this," he told Joe. "I just can't. I'm not hungry any more."

Joe looked at him, puzzled, and Vince slowly began repeating his conversation with Rick. Joe was enjoying his new role as a producer at DreamVision, and he was excited to see what was developing with the story in Russia. But as Vince relayed his conversation with Rick, Joe realized that the ending to this story would not come with Nadia's return home. At that point, both men knew they were embarking upon a much greater adventure than they had previously imagined.

Rick hung up the phone and continued to watch the families play in the park. He prayed for the miracle that would bring Nadia home with him, but also prayed for guidance. It seemed so clear to him now that his purpose extended far beyond simply bringing his new daughter into his life; the faces of the children he had seen in the orphanages were so deeply etched upon his heart and his mind that he knew he'd never forget them.

He returned to the hotel, where he and Stephanie again cried together. Rick called Ed, hoping that perhaps Ed had heard something that would change what now seemed like the inevitable.

Ed could hear the devastation in Rick's voice the moment he picked up the phone. In the months of working together, Rick had become more than a client; Ed had come to regard him as a dear friend and it tugged at Ed's heart to hear Rick in such obvious distress.

"I don't want to leave her," Rick sobbed into the phone. "I can't do this! I have to bring her home!"

"Rick, you have to listen to me," Ed answered, speaking in a low, soothing tone, as if he were approaching a scared or wounded animal. "I know this doesn't seem fair and I know it's difficult. But if you want to make this work, you have to do this their way. You have to follow their rules."

Ed didn't vocalize his true concern; he knew that if Rick tried too hard to interfere with standard procedure that the entire adoption could fall through. He had seen a handful of instances where new parents had, with the best of intentions, tried to expedite the adoption, only to have the entire process be withdrawn. International adoptions could fall apart at any point in the procedure and for the slightest of reasons, and Ed warned Rick that he needed to just come home and wait.

"I feel like I'm abandoning her all over again – I can't let her go through that!" Rick protested.

"It will be okay, Rick," Ed promised. "But this is where your faith is tested, in God and in yourself. You've got to let it go and just come home."

Rick was devastated as he hung up the phone. He had so believed there would be a way for he and Stephanie to get on the train with Nadia the next day. It broke his heart to think of returning without her, so instead he hung to the hope that refused to be extinguished in his heart.

Rick and Stephanie spent a torturously long, sleepless night waiting for morning to come. It seemed like such a cruel fate, to be so close to Nadia and yet be preparing to board a train that would take them even farther away from her. Rick waited for the phone to ring, waited for some last-minute miracle that would let her return home with them. It never came.

Ludmilla and Katarina arrived in the afternoon to take Rick and Stephanie to the train station. The mood was somber and the air was thick with the couple's sorrow as they pulled into the station.

"Please Ludmilla, do whatever you can," Rick begged as they stood on the platform. "We have to come back. I have to get my baby."

Ludmilla nodded, understanding his plight but also knowing the obstacles they were up against. She touched his arm.

"I will do all I can, Mr. Silanskas. But you understand ..."

Rick nodded.

"I know. But please, please Ludmilla..."

Katarina watched their interaction as she hugged Stephanie goodbye. As Ludmilla approached Stephanie, the Katarina whispered something to Ludmilla, who nodded, then turned to hug Stephanie.

"She says she is very worried for your husband, Mrs. Silanskas. Please watch out for him."

Stephanie nodded.

"Thank-you, Ludmilla. Thank-you for all you've done."

"I will do what I can, Mrs. Silanskas. I promise you."

The train was now waiting for them to board. Stephanie and Rick looked at one another, reluctant to take even one more step away from Nadia's world. Ludmilla gently encouraged them to board, and they sullenly took her advice.

As they reached their compartment and stowed their luggage, Rick kept one eye on the open door. He could not bear the thought of closing the door on this world, wanting to stay in it as long as possible. Stephanie reached over to close the door.

"Don't," he begged. "Leave it open. I – I can't. Not yet."

They sat alone in their compartment, clinging tightly to one another, staring at the open door until the conductor came by and closed the door for them. The "click" as the door latched echoed through Rick's head, threatening to detonate the emotions welling within him. He took a tighter grip on Stephanie's hand as she clutched his arm.

"Stephanie, I gotta go get her," he said, the panic rising inside of him. As the locomotive lurched forward on the track, Rick felt as though his heart would come through his chest.

"NO! I can't leave her! I can't leave my baby," he cried, running to the door of their compartment. The train continued picking up speed and Rick knew that his fate was sealed. He fell to his knees and begged God to intervene, asked Him to stop the train and let them return to the orphanage to retrieve Nadia. The train continued down the tracks.

His sobs shook his entire body. Stephanie crumpled into her seat, equally distraught as the grief collided with her exhaustion. Rick ran to the window, hitting it with the heel of his hand.

"I just want to kick the window out of this train," he yelled through his tears. "I just want to go get my baby!"

Each second took them farther away from the reason they had come there, and the suffering that overcame them seemed too great to bear. Rick shook from the physical manifestations of his heartbreak, and he and Stephanie huddled together, two parents grieving for the loss of their child.

As night fell, the train eventually rocked them to sleep as it sped through the Russian terrain. The next thing Rick knew, he awoke in total blackness. He felt as though he were drowning and as he gasped for air, he was certain that he was dying. Suddenly, Stephanie's face appeared before him. He felt her hand on his arm, pulling him back to reality.

He sat up straight, hyperventilating and still struggling for air. Stephanie calmed him, held onto him as he fought to breathe normally through his panic.

"I can't do this, Steph!"

She looked at him, her eyes full of love and concern.

"Listen to me, Rick. Just listen. We have to go through this. We have to go through every second of this to understand it. God has something more for us, but for some reason – we have to endure this first, or we'll never know what others go through."

Rick knew that her words were true, but it did little to ease his grief. He, too, knew that God had more work for him to do in Russia. Rick pulled out his notebook and began writing, filling line after line with thoughts of what he needed to accomplish. Rick wrote for two hours, and as he wrote he developed a vision of what he needed to do for The Project Anna Foundation, of how he needed to begin assisting orphans and what role each of the players on his team should assume.

As Rick and Stephanie sat on the train, rocking gently back and forth with the motion of their car, Rick's mind traveled back over the events of the past few months. She was such a miracle, such a beautiful testament to God's goodness. He again started writing in his notebook.

> *One night, I had a dream*, he wrote.
> *And there I was on the far side of the world.*
> *And suddenly you were there*
> *So small ... alone and frightened*
> *You looked into my heart and my soul*
> *I picked you up and held you in my arms*
> *You were safe ... you were loved ... then you were gone...*

As the emotion swelled within him, so did the music he heard in his mind.

> *I'll never know how He showed me where you were*
> *I would have searched a lifetime*
> *And there you were ... you already knew my heart ...*
> *Then you called me Papa*
> *A dream ... a vision ...it doesn't matter what it's called*
> *You are a miracle*
> *A miracle of His love*

The words poured out of Rick and onto the page, and it seemed as if they were falling directly from his heart onto the paper, not even pausing to register in his mind as he wrote.

> *In my heart there was a space*
> *Especially for you*
> *He carved it with His own hands*
> *Somehow he knew*

I'd search the whole world over
'Til He showed me where you were
Then you walked into the room
My little one ... our little girl

His words were the most profound expression of love imaginable, the pure, unabashed love of a parent for a child. Rick felt such loss without her by his side, yet also felt such gratitude that she was in their hearts and lives forever.

Now sleep my little one, he concluded.
You'll never be alone
Our miracle
Miracle of His love.

Rick's pen stopped, having filled the page with the thoughts of his heart. He didn't know how he would get through the next few weeks or months. Even without her, he knew with certainty that he was only just beginning to grasp the breadth of God's purpose for his life. Nadia, he now knew, was just the beginning.

The little sleep they had gotten on the train had done nothing to rejuvenate them. Alex was waiting for them at the train station and he rushed them to the airport to catch the sixteen-hour flight home. Rick felt helpless as he sat in the plane, and he begged God to give him strength. Suddenly, it felt as if the hands of a loving father had wrapped around him and he was filled with a purposeful sense of calm. He became acutely aware of the blessings that had been bestowed upon him, while at the same time knowing he was being prepared for an awesome and powerful mission.

"God, I'm not good enough for this," he prayed. "There's no way I could do all that you're asking me to do. I have sin in my life and I'm so far from perfect..."

I didn't call you because you're perfect, I called you because you listen.

The voice was as clear as if it had come from Stephanie, who sat beside him. He looked around to see if anyone else had heard the voice. The rest of the passengers seemed oblivious. Rick exhaled, leaned back in his seat and tried to get some sleep.

Stephanie had spoken to Tony on the phone the night before and had warned him about his father's fragile emotional state. Tony greeted his parents with a hug as they arrived at the Orlando airport, and he was concerned by Rick's appearance. Rick looked as if he hadn't slept the entire time he was gone, and his eyes were rimmed in red from crying. Tony kept the mood upbeat as he helped load the luggage into the car. Rick climbed into the back seat as Stephanie took her place beside her son in the front.

"Hey, Dad, I brought you something," Tony said, handing Rick his favorite bottled iced tea. Rick smiled at him, grateful to have a son who was so concerned for him. Rick didn't want to place his own burdens upon his children, but at the same time he was consumed with grief. As they made the ninety-minute drive to their home in Lady Lake, Rick could think of nothing besides Nadia.

It felt as if his heart had been pulled from his chest, and he ached with an emptiness that was even worse than when he had first been looking for her. Now that he had touched her, looked into her eyes and heard her tiny voice, he felt as if there was no greater torture than being separated from her.

Jessica and Andrew greeted them back at the house. Rick and Stephanie's two younger children walked a fine line between giving their parents affection and giving them some space. Their parents were clearly exhausted, both physically and emotionally, but Rick was visibly more shaken by the experience. He felt as if he was caught in some sort of limbo between the world he wanted to be in and the world he was trapped in. Time could not move fast enough and nothing could ease his suffering; all he wanted was to get his baby back.

Every time he closed his eyes, Rick could see her face. He could see her eyes pleading with him to take her home, could feel the gentle beat of her heart. It seemed so unfair to have finally found this little girl, but now have to endure yet another indefinite separation from her.

He and Stephanie collapsed into bed, exhausted.

"Maria has a dance competition tomorrow in Tampa," Stephanie remembered, and Rick sighed. Tampa was about two hours away, which, given the fact that they had just traveled halfway around the world, didn't seem that far. But Rick's body ached from lack of sleep and he wanted nothing more than to crawl in bed and hide away from the world.

"We need to go," he said. "It's important to her that we're there to see her."

Stephanie nodded, but also knew that her schedule would be full of housebound activities after nearly a week away.

"I have some things I have to get done here," she said.

"I'll go. Let's just get some sleep for now."

They laid in the dark, with Rick praying while the tears streamed down his face. He could see her before him, and as he slipped into a fitful sleep, Nadia's face was the last thing he saw.

After a good night's sleep evaded him, Rick crawled from bed the next day still felt depleted. He thought about not attending Maria's recital, but realized it would hardly be fair to ignore one daughter by being consumed of thoughts with another child. He could not forget the family that was here with him. He also knew his support meant so much to his oldest daughter.

Rick grabbed the camera, kissed Stephanie goodbye and began the drive. Having noted Rick's frazzled appearance, Stephanie called Maria in advance to warn her.

"Your father's a mess," she cautioned, "but he's coming anyway."

Maria had inherited many of her father's characteristics, including his tendency to be caught up in the emotions of an event. She felt that she had a good understanding of Rick, relating to him in a way that many others couldn't.

Rick arrived at Maria's ballroom dancing competition just before she took the floor. He marveled at her gracefulness as he watched her sail around the room. It was a firm reminder of how richly God had blessed his life; he already had a beautiful, loving family that he was willing to lay down his life for. The fact that God had chosen to bestow yet another remarkable daughter on him was beyond his comprehension. With that thought, Rick found himself momentarily comforted.

Maria greeted him after her performance, suggesting that they go have lunch after the competition ended. Two hours later they found themselves sitting across from one another in a Tampa restaurant. Maria looked tenderly into Rick's reddened eyes. She had so many questions about Nadia, so much she wanted to know about their trip, but she also knew that her father was hurting. He needed to deliver the information in his own time and on his own terms.

Rick shared pictures from the family's digital camera, showing Maria what her new sister looked like. Watching Nadia was both cathartic and painful; he couldn't get enough of her, yet it was agonizing to see her and think of her being alone.

"I feel like I abandoned her, Maria. She was just looking at me with those big sad eyes as they took her away. I need to get her back, and I can't..."

The turmoil within Rick began bubbling to the surface. His pain erupted with volcanic force, spilling out in tearful reflections. He explained how hard it was to leave her behind, to let go of the child that he had struggled so hard to find. Rick had been so sure that he would be able to bring Nadia home with him and now, sitting here in Florida with empty arms, felt like a cruel joke.

Maria was flooded with compassion for her father. She had seen him in varying states of emotional wreckage during the course of her life, but nothing compared to the kind of suffering he was enduring at the moment. She was both pained for him and completely proud of him.

"You know," she began, speaking slowly and measuring her words. "What you're doing is such a wonderful thing. Look at the difference that you're making in her life.

"I know that it is so hard for you to leave her now, but look at the difference it will make. If you look at the big picture, this really isn't a very long time to be without her, and then she'll be here forever."

Rick nodded, knowing what Maria said was true but still feeling inconsolable. His mind burned with images of children growing up in poverty and neglect, facing a grim and ill-fated future. He began telling Maria about what he had seen in the orphanages of Russia, about the conditions of the buildings and the lack of some of life's basic necessities.

Rick had seen people in various stages of need throughout his life; his volunteer work at homeless shelters had given him what he considered a rather thorough overview of man's most desperate moments. However, none of those experiences had prepared him for what awaited him at the orphanages in Russia; room after room of children being raised with little hope and even fewer of life's bare essentials.

At one of the orphanages, he had been amazed to see that the well from which the children drew their water was at the bottom of a steep hill. Each day, regardless of the weather, they had to carry their buckets down the hill and fill them with water, then struggle together to drag the buckets back up to the orphanage. Rick saw children who were abandoned by parents who could no longer afford to care for them; in some instances, parents would surrender their children to the orphanage simply to know that the child would have a bed to sleep in at night. Some parents returned regularly to visit, others left with the best intentions of returning and never did. It did not matter how the children had arrived there; whether they had been brought by their parents or discovered on the street, the one thing they had in common was a hunger for love, and Rick saw it in every pair of eyes that looked up at him.

His heart seemed to bleed as he broke down, telling Maria what he had seen and how profoundly it had affected him. He could never again go to bed at night without praying for those children, would never again sit down to eat a meal without being conscious of the many children who were eating nothing but bread.

Maria's own eyes filled with tears as her father talked. She was in her final year of college and was studying to be an elementary teacher, a direct reflection of her own adoration for children. To hear

Rick's descriptions of the desperate conditions he had witnessed tugged at her heart.

"Dad, I couldn't do what you're doing," she began, at first fumbling for the right words. She already knew that he was committing his life to helping those children. Perhaps Maria knew it even before Rick had become fully aware of his next mission.

"I can't stand to think about it," Rick said. "All those children, Maria – they're suffering in ways that you and I can't imagine. I can't close my eyes without seeing them. They're all so sad. I want to help them all and I don't know how."

Maria realized that he would find a way to help the children, but at the moment, it was Rick who needed comforted.

"Dad, I can't imagine how hard this is for you. I can't even begin to imagine what you've seen," she said.

"But listen to me. You can't always help everyone. Maybe for right now, Nadia is the only child you can help, but you know what? For that one child, what you're doing is everything. You have at least made a world of difference in her life. And even though it's just one step, it's a step in the right direction."

Rick looked across the table at his oldest child, who had grown into such a beautiful young woman almost overnight. It seemed like only yesterday that he had held her in his arms and he and Stephanie had tearfully rejoiced in the birth of their healthy, perfect first-born. She was the nurturer, the mother hen who cared for her younger brothers and sister, who guided them through the waters she had already navigated, cautioning them about rough patches that laid in wait for them.

From the beginning, Maria had been unusually aware of the world around her, and had always been sensitive to the hurts and needs of others. Now, at a time when Rick needed her most, she was able to use that compassion to ease his aching heart.

Rick felt his resolve strengthening within himself, despite the longing and despair he felt over missing Nadia. He knew with certainty that he had to do something for those other children in Russia. He knew that his mission could not end with bringing Nadia home.

As he and Maria parted ways, Rick pulled his daughter into his arms and hugged her tightly.

"Thank you," he said, his voice barely above a whisper.

"I love you, Dad," she returned, sensing that he was about to expand the journey that he was leading their family on, but at the same time realizing there was no way to predict where it might take them.

Maria had been amazed by the events that had rewritten their family history in the past four months. Like all of the members of the Silanskas crew, she was no stranger to miracles, but knew from the beginning that this was something incredible, even by their standards. She had watched from afar as Rick and Stephanie's dreams of quiet companionship that follows a well-raised family had been traded in on the sole mission of finding and adopting the little girl from the dream. And now, as she watched her father leave, she had no doubts that his early-morning dream in December had been just the beginning.

As Rick made the return trip to his home in Lady Lake, his heart and mind were overflowing. He marveled at how richly he had been blessed by having Maria as his daughter. She was wise beyond her years and sensitive to the emotions of those around her, and Rick offered thanks to God for Maria's ability to touch him in a way that was both comforting and empowering.

Just as he had known on the train ride from Pskov to Moscow, he was being reminded that he had work to do. He did not have the luxury of wallowing in the pain of his separation. Now it was time for Rick to get to work. The problems he had seen in Russia seemed infinite and insurmountable, and it would take an act of God to provide a better life for those children. But Rick had seen plenty of acts of God in his life, and he knew now that he was being called into action. Somewhere down inside him, Rick felt a sense of strength replacing his grief-induced faintness.

Maria's words resonated within him, and now he felt ready to take on a fresh battle, this time fighting for the lives of those children who had touched his heart so deeply.

Rick's purpose behind creating The Project Anna Foundation was to provide aid to families who wanted to adopt Russian orphans, but found the cost prohibitive. Now, having seen the conditions the children lived in, and having learned of how gravely the odds are stacked against them, Rick turned his attention to providing immediate relief for the hundreds of thousands of children housed by the state.

Rick was consumed by the dire need of the orphans in general and Nadia in particular. He was concerned by the lack of medical supplies available to help his ailing child, and it was mind-numbingly painful to think of that situation being multiplied and played out every day by the thousands.

"We've got to help those children," he told Vince, trying to describe the desperation he had seen in the little eyes that looked up at him in each and every orphanage they visited. "I can't walk away from them. We've got to do something."

His first plan of action was to get immediate help for Nadia and the other children in the Pechory baby home. All of the children there were under the age of four, so Rick's first plan of action was to locate a contact for diaper manufacturer Kimberly-Clarke in Moscow. His order for ten thousand Pampers and several boxes of ointment was delivered to Nadia's orphanage the next day. Rick then began working on plans to ease suffering for children in other homes.

As he related story after story of what he had seen children enduring, everyone around him could physically see the changes that had occurred to him during his trip. Rick was both despondent over having to say goodbye to Nadia and determined not to let the orphans be overlooked; within three days of his return, Rick was a man on fire.

He and Stephanie visited with family members the weekend after they returned. The page of the calendar had turned to May, but it seemed an insufferable amount of time until June or July, when Rick and Stephanie would be called back to finalize the adoption. Rick's family could see the pain etched on his face, but knew there was nothing they could do to take that pain from him. He was clearly heartbroken, and as concerned as Carmelita had been for her son while he was gone, she now wanted nothing more than for him to be able to return to Russia to retrieve the adorable little girl in the pictures he showed them.

Dianne had watched her older brother go through heartaches before, but had never seen him as devastated as he was by leaving behind his future daughter. She knew his pattern in such times was simply to shut himself off from the world around him, to disappear and spend time alone with his thoughts and with God. Her concern now was that he would become completely despondent and unavailable. She was surprised over the next few weeks as she realized he was taking a different path this time.

Rick wanted nothing more than to hide himself away, but also knew that he had far too much to accomplish. For Dianne, it was a tremendous testimony to her brother's steadfastness, giving his story and faith even more credibility. It would have been easy for Rick to have faith if God had moved mountains and allowed him to walk out of the orphanage with Nadia in his arms, but now, when his pleas had not been answered, came the true test of his faith. She was proud of him as she watched Rick remain unwavering in his faith and resolute in his course of action. Rick knew it was time for him to get back to work, and he also knew that his life's work had changed forever.

Chapter Twelve

Even before Rick and Stephanie had left Russia, Ludmilla was concerned for Rick's physical and emotional well being. She was accustomed to seeing sadness; she gazed into it every day in the eyes of the orphans she worked with, and lived with it in a way that only those who have known great loss could understand. But Rick's grief was a different kind of pain. While most of the children she tried to comfort wrestled with the absence of hope in their lives, Rick's source of distress was the heart-breaking anguish of separation.

Nadia's remarkable story had touched Ludmilla from the first time she heard it. The orphanage workers in Pechory had told her the amazing story of an American man who had dreamed about a little Russian child and had even drawn a picture of what that child looked like. It was a miracle almost too great to believe when that child turned out to be in their orphanage, and from the moment Ludmilla met Rick and Stephanie in their train compartment, she could feel his compassion.

His concern had not ended with Nadia, and that touched Ludmilla's heart even more deeply. She was accustomed to seeing adoptive parents who traveled to Russia and, although most were shaken by what they saw at the orphanage, they rarely expressed a desire or need to help.

Rick and Stephanie were different. She knew that as she took them from one orphanage to the next and watched the tears well up in Rick's eyes. The couple asked countless questions about the children, wanting to know where they got their food and what became of the children as they grew into young adults. Ludmilla's answers were straightforward and bleak; each answer seemed to pierce more deeply into Rick's aching heart. He obviously loved Nadia very much, but in his search for one child, he had now somehow fallen in love with an entire country of children.

Ludmilla wasn't sure how well Rick would fare after leaving Nadia behind. It had been heartbreaking to watch the couple as the baby was taken from their arms and returned to the room with the other children. The pain seemed too great for him to bear, and as he pleaded with Ludmilla to help him, she felt as helpless as she did each time she looked upon a room full of children hoping desperately that their parents would walk through the orphanage doors.

After Rick's return to America, Ludmilla continued making regular visits to see Nadia. Each time, she carried pictures of Rick and Stephanie along with her, reminding Nadia that they were her Mama and Papa. Ludmilla e-mailed frequent reports of those visits back to Rick, who could not seem to escape the sadness brought by the separation.

"Please, Ludmilla, please, whatever you can do," he would beg her over the phone, the tears audible in his voice. "I have to get her now. She has suffered so much; I can't bear the thought of her sitting there alone."

Each call was heartbreaking for Ludmilla, and every e-mail Rick sent reminded her of the couple's pain. Just a week after he had returned to his Florida home, Rick e-mailed Ludmilla a lengthy letter detailing his feelings for his daughter and the desperate longing he felt without her. He poured his heart out through his computer keyboard, telling Ludmilla of how profoundly the experiences in Russia had changed him. It was a powerful, emotional piece of writing, as lyrical as anything Rick had ever composed at a piano and as emotionally stirring as a symphony.

Ludmilla read the letter again and again; each time it brought tears to her eyes. She wanted so much to help this intriguing and compassionate man. As she read the letter again, Ludmilla knew, without a shadow of a doubt, what she must do.

A single judge handles the international adoptions for the region, and Ludmilla knew the judge to be a kind, good-hearted woman. Ludmilla translated Rick's e-mail into Russian, then made an appointment to visit the judge in her chambers.

"He is a special man," Ludmilla explained as she presented the judge with a translated version of Rick's letter. Ludmilla told the unique story, beginning with Rick's dream and his tireless search to find the little girl that he held briefly in his arms before waking. She told of the picture he had used to find Nadia, told of the miracle of Nadia's face appearing on the web site the very day his home had been approved for adoption. Finally, she told of Rick's heartbreak over leaving this child behind and the distress he felt for all the children of Russia.

As she finished talking, Ludmilla noticed that the judge had been visibly touched by the story she had just heard.

"Alright, what can I do for you?" the judge asked with unusual softness.

"Can we get him a court date – soon?" Ludmilla pleaded.

The judge opened her book, scanning page after page of dates filled with hearings. No openings existed before June; each hearing was a lengthy process, so the judge normally only heard two cases a day.

Ludmilla looked at her hopefully as the judge scanned the pages again.

"What about May 26?" Ludmilla suggested, knowing the date was only two weeks away.

"I already have two court dates scheduled on that day."

Ludmilla felt her hopes and her heart sinking.

The judge sighed. "But what else can I do? I will have the third."

Ludmilla was elated, knowing that whether Rick and Stephanie realized it or not, another small miracle had just occurred for them; opening a door in the Russian courts is usually much harder to budge. She returned home that evening, recounting the events to Rick and Stephanie in an e-mail.

"So prepare to come to Russia again," she wrote, telling them that permission for their return already had been sent to the Russian Embassy in New York, allowing them to travel back May 23 through June 5. The court date was set for May 26, and after a mandatory ten-day waiting period, they would be able to return home with Nadia if the adoption was approved.

Rick read Ludmilla's e-mail, both stunned and overjoyed as the words registered in his mind. Only ten days had passed since he and Stephanie had returned home, but each day had seemed to drag on like months. Now, to already have a date in place for them to see Nadia again, was nothing short of a prayer come true. The open-ended waiting was over; he finally knew with certainty that he would have his daughter in his arms again in two weeks.

The house was ready for Nadia's return home, and excitement bubbled throughout it as the entire family counted down the days until her return. Excitement was tangible wherever Rick went; whether he was at home or at the office, every thought now revolved around his little girl. He continued pouring ideas and energy into The Project Anna Foundation, determined now not to let his miracle end with Nadia's adoption.

In many ways, the return trip to Russia seemed much the same as it had been a month earlier; the family gathered around the car and wished them a safe trip before Tony drove Rick and Stephanie to the Orlando International Airport. But this time, the lengthy trip had a different sense of anticipation. Now, they both had held Nadia, and they had the same nervous energy of any parent who is seeing a child after a separation of any kind, whether it's a first day of school or a week away at summer camp.

It was interesting for Rick to watch the Russian countryside through the window of the train again. He thought about his first trip to the country, recalled the sense of excitement and wonder he had felt as he looked upon these sights with the eyes of a stranger. Then, as he had returned from Pskov to Moscow under the cloak of the night, the countryside had seemed to swallow up the train they were riding in. Rick had felt so lost and alone on that return trip, so completely heartbroken by leaving Nadia behind. It made his heart leap to think about returning with her, and he knew that the ride would seem much shorter with the child sharing their train compartment.

Ludmilla again greeted the couple as the train pulled into the station in Pskov. The three adults were overjoyed at seeing one another, hugging each other warmly as they met. This was the part of her job that sustained Ludmilla, seeing loving couples return to be reunited with the child they had fallen in love with. She was fond of Rick and Stephanie, felt more of an attachment to them than she typically shared with couples. They seemed to have so much love to give and seemed so willing to share it with all those they met; it was rare to meet people so genuinely determined to help the well-being of others.

The first order of business was to return to Nadia's orphanage. After long days of waiting, the minutes seemed to grind to a halt and the hour-long drive felt longer than ever before. Rick and Stephanie were bursting with love and excitement as they returned through the shabby doors of the orphanage. Moments later, Nadia returned in the arms of an orphanage caregiver.

She seemed to grow more beautiful each time they laid eyes on her. Any concerns that she might have forgotten this couple vanished as Nadia's eyes rested on Rick and Stephanie. Nadia was happy to see them, and as they were reunited, Ludmilla felt tears filling her eyes. To see Nadia so relaxed and happy made Ludmilla ecstatic. She knew with complete certainty that this little girl had a wonderful life before her.

The three played together for about an hour, and to Rick it felt as if they had never been apart. As was customary, an official for the orphanage observed the interaction and would be at the court hearing the following day to provide input as to how the adoption should proceed. Sometimes, children are frightened by the adults who visit them, particularly the men, so an official is always on hand before the court proceeding to make sure both sides were comfortable with one another.

Watching them play together, Ludmilla was certain that the adoption hearing would proceed smoothly. They seemed to be a family that was joined as naturally as if Nadia had been born to Rick and Stephanie.

This time, leaving Nadia was hard, but the air was filled with a joyous sense of the impending reunion. Rick and Stephanie tearfully handed her back to the orphanage worker and watched her disappear behind those doors, knowing it was the last time they would ever have to tell her goodbye. It filled both of their hearts with joy to realize that the next time they visited Nadia, it would be to bring her home for good.

They held hands as they walked out to the car. Rick's enthusiasm and excitement was tempered with sorrow for all the children that would be left behind. He looked up at the orphanage's upstairs window and again saw that the curtain had been pulled away. Little hands pressed against the window, and little eyes peered out. It was a heart-wrenching sight. Rick released a heavy sigh.

"Boy, Steph, we really have to do something for them," he said. She nodded, knowing that the sights and plights of these children now were indelibly burned into his heart. As they drove back to the hotel in Pskov, they were able to catch up with Ludmilla and learn more about what they could expect from the hearing the next day. Just as it had been with the first visit, they were filled with a nervous uncertainty. It was one thing to understand what the official proceedings would be, but it was quite another to go through them. It was much like getting married, Rick thought. No amount of preparation can truly get one ready for that moment of joy. Many of the feelings he had now were much like the ones he had felt as he prepared for his wedding day. It was a joyous kind of anxiety, a sort of positive apprehension that he knew would culminate in one of the happiest moments of his life.

Rick and Stephanie thought the night would never end, and they were ready the next morning long before Ludmilla arrived to take them to court. Ludmilla again explained the procedure as they went to the court, where she would continue serving as their translator.

It was, in many ways, business as usual that day in the Russian courts. A court official read aloud a document declaring that Rick and Stephanie Silanskas had applied for the adoption of the child named Nadezchda, who was a resident of the Pechory Baby Orphanage.

Through Ludmilla, the judge asked Rick and Stephanie if they still supported the application and wished to proceed. The affirmative answer they gave in unison could not have been more emphatic.

Having met with Ludmilla only two weeks earlier, the judge already was familiar with the details of their unusual story. It is customary in adoption proceedings for the judge to ask the parents to speak candidly about their reasons for adopting, and in this case, the judge was more interested than usual in hearing Rick's side of the story. Through Ludmilla, she asked Rick to tell his story for the official court record of the Russian federation.

Slowly, Rick began recounting the events of the past few months. He told of having two dreams about this child in a single night, and of being so moved by what he experienced that he knew it was more than a dream. He told of his desperation to find her, of finding The Open Door Adoption Agency and enlisting them in his mission. And then, after sleepless, restless weeks of searching for her, finally finding Nadia's photo on the Pechory web site. With the passion and emotion rising in his voice, Rick told of his first trip to Russia with Stephanie, and how as Nadia appeared through the doors of the orphanage for the first time, he knew that he was about to hold the exact same child he had held in his dream.

"I physically held that baby in my arms," he told the court, his eyes now growing moist although his voice remained strong and unwavering.

"I don't know how it happened, but I know it did. She *is* a miracle, your honor. And she is my daughter."

Ludmilla cleared her throat, fighting back the lump that was growing in it as she heard Rick's words and translated them into Russian. She looked at the judge, who was wiping back tears; Ludmilla then looked at the prosecutor, who also had tears in his eyes. Behind her, she could hear sniffling, and she realized that there wasn't a dry eye in the courtroom.

The judge took a moment to regain her composure, then thanked Rick for his words. She turned her attention to Stephanie and asked her, as a mother, to speak from her heart about the child they were about to adopt.

Accustomed to playing the steadfast rock, Stephanie stood and began to speak. But the emotions she was usually able to keep in check now overwhelmed her, and tears began flowing as freely as the words that spilled from her lips.

She explained that she and Rick had not been looking for another child, but when Rick told her of his dream, she knew that their lives were about to change. Nadia already had become a part of them, and they had prayed for her health and safety from the moment that dream occurred.

Stephanie talked of her anguish at leaving Nadia behind, and expressed the joy she felt at their reunion.

"Your honor, I know that God sent this child to us," she said through her tears. "And I know that I will love her and protect her until the day I die."

As Stephanie took her seat, silence fell across the courtroom, punctuated only by the sniffling of those in the courtroom. The judge shuffled some papers as she again sought her composure. She then asked for the orphanage director to provide the court with the official state history of the child.

Rick and Stephanie knew vague bits and pieces of Nadia's past, but they had not yet heard her entire story. They clasped hands and listened intently as Ludmilla translated the orphanage director's words.

Nadezchda, or Nadia, had been in the care of the Pechory Baby Orphanage since she was about six months old, they learned. She had been left alone in a home about two hundred kilometers from Pechory. The officials who discovered the little girl had delivered her to the baby orphanage.

Officials searched for the baby's mother, knowing that without her signature, this child could never be adopted. They spent a year looking for her, but were unable to find her. Finally, they located her in a hospital, her body racked with illness and her health failing quickly. She willingly signed away her parental rights, making Nadia eligible for adoption, on the morning of December 23, 2002.

Stephanie's jaw dropped as she heard the story. She asked Ludmilla to request the orphanage director to repeat the date.

"December 23, 2002, after a year of searching, her mother signed her rights over and Nadezchda became eligible for adoption," Ludmilla repeated back to her as the orphanage director re-read the paperwork.

Stephanie gasped and she and Rick looked at one another in amazement.

"Mrs. Silanskas, is something wrong?" the judge asked.

"That's the date that my husband had his dream," Stephanie stammered. "He had his dream about her on the morning of December 23."

The emotion that had subsided with the official reading from the orphanage director now began to fill the room again.

"Mrs. Silanskas," the judge asked through Ludmilla, "can you tell me what time this dream took place?"

"About three a.m."

The judge looked at the papers and exhaled heavily. Tears spilled down her cheeks and her usually commanding voice wavered as she spoke. She explained that the documents had been signed around eleven a.m. in Russia. Given the eight-hour time difference between Florida and Russia, it was clear that Rick's dream occurred at the very hour Nadia's mother was signing the paperwork.

Now the sniffling from others in the courtroom was breaking into sobs, as all those who listened to the story found themselves touched by the incredible story they had just witnessed. Just when they thought they knew all there was to know about their miraculous child, Rick and Stephanie had received even greater evidence of God's greatness at work.

The judge closed her book of documents and announced that she was dismissing the normal order of the courtroom, and that everyone was allowed to speak freely. She turned her attention to Rick and Stephanie. Through Ludmilla, she asked them to approach the bench.

Rick had brought along a picture book that he and Stephanie had assembled specifically for this occasion. They showed the judge pictures of them at various stages of their life together, showed pictures of their children and their home and their pets. She looked at his photos in amazement, tears flowing from her eyes, overwhelmed by what she had witnessed that day in her own courtroom.

"You have given us so much hope today, Mr. and Mrs. Silanskas," she told them through Ludmilla. "For that, on behalf of the Russian people, I thank you."

Rick felt as if his heart would burst with emotion. He was standing in a courtroom in a foreign country where he was a stranger who didn't speak the language, yet he felt completely loved and accepted. Even more importantly, he felt a love for all of the people in the room with him. His heart filled with gratitude, not just for the daughter God had led him to, but for the new understanding and compassion he had for a country he'd never before given a second thought to.

The judge called the court back to order to offer her official decree. She wiped the tears from her eyes and cleared her throat. When she spoke, her words were steady and measured, a heartfelt declaration that Ludmilla translated to Rick and Stephanie.

"Mr. and Mrs. Silanskas, I cannot argue with God," she said.

"What God has done is now official in the Russian federation. Take your child. There will be no ten-day waiting period. You may take this child home."

Rick and Stephanie both released cries of joy and relief. They pulled Ludmilla into a tearful, grateful hug with them. Ludmilla felt her heart leaping with a joy she had never known; she believed in miracles, even though she lived in a country where they seemed even harder to come by than a loaf of bread. But she had lived through this miracle, had seen it unfold and had walked through it at Rick and Stephanie's side. She knew it was a story she would tell over and over again for the rest of her life.

They spent the rest of the day filling out the necessary paperwork. It was, in many ways, maddening for Rick and Stephanie; all they wanted now was to be able to return to the orphanage and Pechory to take Nadia away once and for all. But they plowed through the mountain of documents, knowing that each signature took them one step closer to holding their daughter again.

Ludmilla arrived at their hotel early the next morning, and Rick and Stephanie were eagerly waiting for her. They had been too excited to get a good night's sleep, and their buoyancy would carry them through the next several days as well. As they neared the orphanage, Rick could feel his heart leaping with joy. She was so, so close – at last!

They passed the monastery and turned onto the now-familiar dirt road that led them to Nadia. Rick remembered the first time he had seen this road, recalled how his legs had felt like jelly. Now, it seemed as if his heart would soar out of his chest.

Rick and Stephanie climbed the metal stairs behind Ludmilla, barely able to contain their emotions. Rick wanted to fly up those stairs, wanted these last few excruciating seconds that stood between them and Nadia to disappear forever. They entered the orphanage's waiting area, the same room where they had seen Nadia for the very first time. The orphanage director greeted them warmly, happy and relieved to see such a wonderful new beginning for Nadia.

She explained that the children were all being prepared for their naps and called Nadia's caregiver to the front desk. She explained Rick and Stephanie were ready to take Nadia home now.

"Come back with us," they motioned for Rick and Stephanie to follow, and as Rick moved toward the doorway, Stephanie stood still.

"I can't go in there," Stephanie told him softly. Her eyes were filled with sorrow, and Rick knew that she was thinking of all the little children in the room they would have to leave behind. It would be impossible for her to turn and leave them there.

Rick nodded, knowing what his wife's eyes were saying. He turned with Ludmilla to follow the orphanage worker down the dark hallway that led to the room filled with children.

Rick entered the room and saw several rows of beds lined up. The room held seventeen tiny beds, and in each bed was a child wearing just their underwear. All seventeen of the little heads popped up in hope and curiosity as the adults entered the room.

Nadia's bed was empty; she was already being dressed by one of the orphanage workers. Rick and Stephanie had brought her clothes the day before; the orphanage required adoptive parents to bring their child clothes because the children shared clothing, so they must leave behind what they wear at the orphanage. As he entered the room, Nadia gave Rick the smile he already had fallen in love with.

"Papa!" she cried out, and he again felt hot tears rimming his eyes. She was so beautiful, so full of life; he couldn't imagine living his life without her in it.

As the workers continued dressing her, all of the other children in the room solemnly watched the process, knowing that Nadia had found a home and was going to leave.

They all look so sad, Rick thought, his joy now tempered with grief for these heartbroken children. They were children who already had learned not to cry out loud, had learned to contain their pain at all costs. The lessons life had handed to them, even at this early stage in their life, had been harsh ones, and they knew better than to get their hopes up. Still, with each arrival of parents came the potential for a better life, and with each departure of another of their friends came deepened disappointment.

He watched as one little girl, who could not have been more than three years old, fixed her gaze on Nadia. She watched every movement of the worker as Nadia was being dressed, and finally she turned to stare, wide-eyed, at Rick. A single tear rolled down her cheek, and at that moment Rick felt it would be impossible to turn and walk from that room.

It felt as if someone had nailed his feet to the floor. He did not want to walk down those stairs until he knew that each and every one of these innocent little faces would be guaranteed a better life.

As he watched the little girl in the bed watching Nadia, a little boy jumped from his bed and ran to Rick.

"Papa!" he cried, wrapping his arms tightly around Rick's leg. Tears rolled down his face, and he was pleading with Rick in Russian to take him instead. Rick's heart broke as the little boy gripped Rick's leg as if his life depended on it. Hearing the commotion, a second orphanage worker entered the room and began slowly prying the boy's fingers from Rick's thigh. Rick began to cry, now feeling overwhelmed by the children's desperation. They were so accustomed to being forgotten, and he renewed his promise to never forget what God had led him to discover.

Nadia now was dressed, smiling, and clutching the floppy stuffed puppy dog that Rick and Stephanie had given her on their first visit. That visit now seemed so long ago; he was amazed at how much had happened in his life and in his heart in such a short time. The worker motioned Rick to come over, and they showed him the closet where her clothes hung. They showed him the bed that had been hers, offering him a brief tour of the life that she was leaving behind. Before he arrived, they told him, Nadia had been walking around with the book of pictures Rick and Stephanie left on their first visit. She had been pointing to their pictures, showing the other children her mama and papa. They said it was as if she was just waiting for Rick and Stephanie to come back.

Rick hugged Nadia to his chest, feeling as if his heart would burst from the combination of love and sorrow. He knew that from this moment forth, there would never be a time when he didn't feel her in his heart, would never be a time when he would forget how this moment felt. It was as powerful as witnessing the birth of his own children. He kissed his daughter, knowing it was time to join Stephanie, who was waiting in the other room.

His legs felt as if they had been weighted down with lead as he walked to the door. Rick felt an attachment and sense of responsibility to every child in that room; walking out, with their little eyes staring sadly at his back, made Rick feel like he was abandoning every one of them.

Rick and Stephanie spent the rest of the day traveling with Nadia, making the long, twelve-hour train ride back to Moscow. After months of being without her, Rick and Stephanie felt joy that surpassed any words or music they had ever heard. Their story was an intricate symphony of emotions, with undercurrents of tragedy driven by a joyous ending. All that they had seen had left Rick and Stephanie sadder and more determined to do something for all of the children who had nothing. Rick promised Ludmilla he would be back, promised that he would return to help more children. His promises stirred her; she believed that somehow he would find a way to make them come true.

Rick had become fascinated with the sights and traditions of this country, and the musician in him was enthralled with the sounds native to Russia. On the train from Pskov to Moscow, he could hear the simple folk sounds of Russia being integrated with the richness of a symphony. As the music came to life within him, Rick began making notes for what would become his next musical project.

In Moscow, Rick and Stephanie showed Nadia a world she had never seen before; her life up until then had been lived in three rooms. Now, they took her around Red Square, showed her the beauty of nature in a way she had never experienced. At the Moscow Zoo, she saw animals she had never seen before and rode on carnival rides. Rick bought her cotton candy, but she was terrified of the strange, fluffy treat on a stick. She fared better at McDonald's, where Rick bought Nadia her first Big Mac and she devoured it as if she hadn't eaten in days.

Rick could see the wonder in her eyes, and each time it took his breath away. It was a time of celebration beyond anything he could describe. He called his family by cell phone, letting each of them say hello to Nadia. Talking to Nadia only heightened his family's excitement as they waited anxiously for Rick and Stephanie to return to Florida with the newest member of the Silanskas brood.

Chapter Thirteen

Inside the terminal at Orlando International Airport, the Silanskas clan anxiously awaited the arrival of Rick, Stephanie and Nadia as they flew in from New York. As they waited for the plane to touch down, family members were filled with the kind of joyous anticipation normally reserved for the waiting room of a maternity ward.

This had been a long journey for every member of the Silanskas family, and each had been touched in a different way. For everyone involved, this had been a testament to faith in action, an amazing test of moving forward despite what conventional wisdom might say.

Less than six months had passed since Rick first dreamed of holding Nadia in his arms, and while it had seemed like an eternity to Rick, it had been nothing short of a fast-moving miracle in the eyes of those who observed it.

At The Open Door Adoption Agency in Georgia, Ed Thomas remained pleasantly surprised by how quickly the events transpired. To him, there was no greater proof of God's handiwork in this matter than to see how quickly walls had dissolved and how doors had opened as they moved forward in their search for the little Russian girl. Nadia had become available quickly, and the red tape that usually surrounded international adoptions seemed to disappear.

The application to be approved for international adoption, which can take up to sixty days to process, had been completed in just three weeks. Although Nadia should not have been available for international adoption until June, she was somehow able to meet her new parents in April. And then, just one month later, she was returning home with Rick and Stephanie. Nothing about this adoption was what could be termed "run of the mill," and to those who had witnessed the events unfolding, it seemed certain that this was only the beginning.

Even the Russian press had been amazed by the story. While still in Russia to complete Nadia's paperwork, Rick and Stephanie were contacted by a reporter for the Pskov newspaper. The story detailed the events of Rick's dream and the search that followed; even in print, this turn of events was heralded as "a sign from God." Rick and Stephanie were overwhelmed by how openly their story was being declared a miracle; the official court record of Russia noted it was an act of God. Those events floored Rick and he realized that he had developed a true connection with this country. It went beyond compassion; he now somehow felt as if he had been led to this land, had been directed to focus his efforts on touching the lives of the people who seemed so badly in need of hope.

As Rick had said goodbye to Ludmilla at the Pskov train station, he had promised that he would return. He knew it was a promise that would be kept at all costs. His words brought tears to her eyes and touched her heart in ways that Rick would never understand. In all her years of working with adoptive parents, no one had ever offered to come back for the sake of the children left behind. Many of the prospective parents went straight from the orphanage to their hotel rooms, not wanting to see the harsh reality facing the Russian people. Ludmilla had seen some parents return to adopt a second child, but this was the first time someone wanted to come back just to help the many children who would never know the safety of a real home.

Everyone who had been involved with the story of Nadia spent time lost in their own thoughts and emotions as Rick and Stephanie were bringing her home. The sixteen-hour flight from Moscow to New York, which had seemed unending on their previous visit, now seemed to take just a fraction of the time. Nadia already had accepted them as "mama" and "papa." Both Rick and Stephanie had felt the wonder and joy of new parents as they awoke that next morning after the final court hearing with Nadia in their hotel room.

It was almost unfathomable that she was finally physically with them, and would be with them forever. The dream that many would think sounded too good to be true had come true in a way that no Hollywood director could have scripted. Rick and Stephanie took turns sitting with Nadia on the plane, watching her as she watched the world for the first time. They marveled at her beauty and perfection, and they reveled in the excitement of all that lay before them.

The entire Silanskas clan had been well-schooled on how to react when Nadia arrived home. Like first-time parents, Rick and Stephanie had pored over manuals and how-to books, learning the ways to make Nadia feel comfortable and safe in her new surroundings. They had cautioned their relatives that she might be shy and had warned them to let little Nadia initiate contact. Everyone would move at Nadia's comfort level, being careful not to over-stimulate or scare the child in her new environment.

The plane taxied into the gate at around eight o'clock on the night of May 31, 2003, excitement building within the entire family as each second ticked off the clock. Waiting at the gate were Rick and Stephanie's four older children, all of whom were eagerly anticipating the arrival of a baby sister. Of the four, Maria had the most concerns; now that she was away at college, and would pursue a career in education after graduation, she worried that little Nadia wouldn't know who she was. It was an unusual role for the eldest child, who had always been the one her siblings turned to for advice or a voice of reason. Since she would be absent more than she would be home, Maria had concerns that her role in her new sister's life would be minimal.

"Make sure you put pictures of me all over the house," she had made Stephanie promise. "I don't want her to forget who I am!"

It would be a different story for the other three children. With his education in film production completed, Tony had returned home and was not only working with his father, but living under Rick and Stephanie's roof once again. It would give him plenty of time to enjoy the kind of bonding that Jessica and Andrew both would have access to. All three of them were excited to begin the next chapter in the family history.

Andrew, who had begged Stephanie for years to give him a younger brother or sister, was getting his wish, while Jessica looked forward to having another girl in the house. They all had contributed eagerly to Nadia's new room, and now wanted to see the little girl for themselves.

Vince and Cris were there with their two children, as were Dianne and John. Rick's parents, Carmelita and Richard, were there, Richard with his video camera in tow, and Jimmy Huckaby was there to film Nadia's arrival for his documentary.

The small knot huddled together in excitement, generating a kind of electricity that was tangible to those who passed them. They scanned the throngs of passengers flowing out of the airport gates, eager to catch the first glimpse of the newest family member.

Andrew was the first to spot his parents.

"Look! There they are!" he said, pointing. The rest of the crew began jumping, waving their arms to catch Rick and Stephanie's attention. The smiles painted across the faces of the new parents said everything that was in their hearts. In Rick's arms was Nadia, the girl of his dreams. She was even more beautiful than the pictures Rick had taken on his last visit, and her big brown eyes seemed to be drinking in the sights and sounds that surrounded her.

As Rick and Stephanie walked toward their family, Nadia began to wave her little hand at her new brothers and sisters. Maria rushed forward and hugged her mother, while Jessica moved toward Rick and Nadia. Nadia looked, wide-eyed at her sister, studying a face that looked so much like her own. The resemblance to the rest of the family was uncanny; she had the same brown eyes and many of the same features of her siblings. It was as if she had been cut from the same cloth and had simply waited for her rightful family to claim her.

Carmelita had anxiously awaited Nadia's return. Not only had her concerns about loving an adopted child disappeared, they had been replaced with a sense of love and compassion for this child even before Carmelita met her. Her heart felt so full of love as she watched her oldest child walking through the airport with her youngest grandchild. The amazement and joy she felt exceeded even the feelings she'd had upon the births of her other grandchildren, and she knew without a doubt that Rick was bringing home a miracle.

She waited as Nadia's brothers and sisters moved in, gently touching Nadia's hand and telling her their names. Then Carmelita moved toward the newest member of the family, unable to keep the tears from slipping down her cheeks. She kissed Nadia, leaned back and gazed upon the child, then kissed her again. It was as if she already knew this child in her heart, and it felt as though she was being reunited with a part of her heart that she had not known was missing.

Slowly, each of her relatives introduced themselves to Nadia and she gazed intently at each one, looking at them with eyes that seemed to understand they were now a part of her life. Rick and Stephanie both were tired from the week of travel and emotions, but also were exuberant at being able to return with Nadia at last. Knowing that their daughter had experienced a tiresome trip as well, they kept the airport celebration brief so they could begin the ninety-minute drive to their home in Lady Lake.

In the car, Nadia was quiet and curious. As they arrived home, Rick carried her upstairs, followed by the rest of the family. They had prepared a room for Nadia, but also knew it was too soon to leave her alone for the night. A small baby bed had been moved into Rick and Stephanie's bedroom, allowing Nadia to share their room until she felt safe enough to spend the night in her own. It would give them the chance to provide Nadia with the nurturing which had been so lacking in her short life, and also allow them to build a stronger bond with their daughter.

Still in wonderment that he was finally holding his daughter in his own home, as Rick placed her in the bed, tucking her in, he leaned over her, wanting her to sleep but not wanting to take his eyes off her. Nadia gazed back at him, then reached over and pushed his head down so that he would be eye-to-eye with her. Rick smiled and kept his head there for a few moments, and as his daughter began drifting off to sleep, he quietly began to move away. Nadia opened her eyes and again pushed his head down beside her own. Rick's heart filled with a sense of love and joy that can only be understood by a parent. Relinquishing to her wish, he left his head next to hers until both of them were finally consumed by the weariness they had managed to keep at bay.

Waking with Nadia in the house seemed to add a sense of buoyancy to the air; Rick and Stephanie were overjoyed to have her home. Rick found himself waking up with the same joy he had known in the second dream he experienced on December 23. In that dream, he had raced up the stairs and discovered the little girl sleeping soundly in her own bed in her own room. Now, he was waking up and finding her happily sleeping in her bed near their own, clutching the little stuffed puppy they had given her on their first visit.

As joyous as Rick was over her presence in their home, he knew that he could not forget what he had seen. He couldn't forget the children who had looked to him, so very desperate for love and hoping against all hope that he would be the one who would take them to a place called home. It broke his heart each time he thought of the tiny faces. He could see the tear-stained face of the little girl who watched Nadia being dressed to leave; he could still feel the grip of the little boy clutching his leg and begging Rick to take him. It all felt like too much for his heart to bear, and his prayers were tearful, fervent pleas for guidance in helping each and every one of the children he had met on his journey.

Even before they had traveled to Russia, Stephanie already had predicted that the experience they were having would not end with Nadia. In one of their many conversations about what was taking place, Stephanie told Rick that she believed God would use each and every one of his talents to touch the children of Russia. As they returned home and began settling back into their routine, Rick realized how true her words were.

The symphony that had begun on the train ride home with Nadia continued to build within his head. It began to take shape in a dramatic way, telling the story of his entire journey while at the same time sharing the story of the children who can not speak for themselves. Rick began taking notes as the symphony continued ringing in his ears. It began with a single, haunting violin solo, something that embodied the pain and loneliness of a single child searching for love.

Each time he heard the violin solo in his head, his heart ached for a young girl he had seen repeatedly on a Moscow street corner. She was just a child, no more than eight or nine years old, and she would stand alone, playing in the cold and waiting for passers-by to toss rubles into the little cup at her feet. When the crowds would thin, she would take a break, running to the shadows of a doorway, where a family member would sit waiting for her to bring the money for safekeeping.

It seemed to Rick as if she let the violin do the weeping that she would not allow herself to do. He was struck by the passion of her music, and haunted by the pain in her eyes. As the symphony began in his head, he could see her playing, one single child providing the voice of thousands.

That single voice would then be joined by dozens of other strings, symbolizing all the children who were no longer alone. Rick poured his heart into his music and the vision for the symphony continued to unfold in his heart. All of the feelings he could never put into words were translated into heartfelt sounds, transformed into notes that were found somewhere so deep within him that he could only weep as he wrote them.

It would take him more than a year to complete the project, which he called "A Symphony of Hope for the Children of Russia." Even before he knew how it would end, he began envisioning the symphony not just as a musical recording, but as a live television broadcast that could cross international boundaries and reach millions of people worldwide. DreamVision already was working on an animated version of the story, and now he wanted to create a feature film as well. He knew that all of these things needed to happen, not just to tell Nadia's incredible story but also to make others aware of the many children who crave the very things that many people take for granted each day. Rick wasn't sure how all of this could be accomplished, nor was he particularly concerned with how those details would fall into place. After all, he felt that God had just led him to a child who was waiting for him on the other side of the world, so it seemed unreasonable to doubt that all the other components would fall into place.

Rick didn't want to make Nadia a poster child for international adoption, but he also did not want to close the door on the many children still there. He and Stephanie prayed daily for the children in Russia, and through The Project Anna Foundation they began to raise money to take back to the orphanages they had visited. Rick now knew this was his next mission in life, and where music once was the singular focus of his career, it now seemed a means to an end. It was a gift designed to allow him to accomplish his true calling in life.

Nadia's first two days in her new home were quiet ones. She seemed relieved each time she woke up, as if she had somehow been afraid this was only a dream and she would soon return to the reality she had known. Although the days were filled with joy, the nights were sometimes torturous for Nadia. She would fall asleep, only to be tormented with ghosts from her past and would awaken screaming and frightened. Rick and Stephanie would rush to her side, holding her and assuring her that she was safe.

It broke Rick's heart to know that she had places in her memory that were so dark, and he knew that her sad story represented the majority of the orphans he had met. He would never know what dark, torturous secrets were haunting his daughter. After two months of watching her endure the traumatic night-time images, Rick held her one night and prayed for her. He asked for the nightmares to vanish and for her heart and mind to be replaced with the love of her new family. It was the last time Nadia experienced a nightmare.

As they taught her their language and introduced her to a brand new life, the Silanskas family watched Nadia being transformed from a quiet little girl into an outgoing and happy child. By her third day, Nadia was eager to play with Jessica and Andrew, happily rolling around on the floor with them and delighting in their care and companionship. From Jessica, she began to learn to dance. She also learned the English language quickly, and before long they couldn't remember a day when she wasn't happily chattering away.

She reminded Rick of a flower, a tiny, neglected bud that had been kept away from the sunlight and water. As they showered her with love and light, she blossomed before their eyes. Each day she seemed to glow brighter than the day before.

Nadia became something of an ambassador of love, greeting everyone she met with an enthusiastic and endearing smile. She was sincerely happy to be alive and just as happy to greet each day.

Stephanie still had not told her family about the child they had adopted or the unusual way in which the adoption had transpired. With her family living in England, she knew it would be a difficult thing to explain. Instead of trying to phone each person and re-tell the story, they waited until Jimmy Huckaby had completed his documentary.

"Nadia's Story" condensed the chain of events into a thirty-minute story. Having filmed the story as it unfolded, Jimmy was able to capture key moments in Rick and Stephanie's journey of faith. To supplement the footage he had shot, Stephanie and Rick provided Jimmy with film footage they had shot during their two trips to Russia.

The documentary was a moving and beautiful piece, one that conveyed both the anticipation and frustration of the search. Jimmy incorporated Armando's original drawing into the footage, and when shown side-by-side with the little girl they found in the orphanage, it removed all doubt as to whether or not it was the same child.

Jimmy ended the documentary with "Miracle of His Love," the song that Rick had written for Nadia on the train ride from Pskov to Moscow. Rick's good friend and co-worker, Kim Shelly, had painstakingly compiled video footage of Rick and Nadia and created the music video as a gift to Rick. The completed effort perfectly illustrated the words Rick had penned.

At the end of July, 2003, Jimmy completed his documentary. Rick made DVDs of "Nadia's Story" and, along with an adoption announcement, sent the documentary to each of Stephanie's family members. It seemed a bit unorthodox, but it also was much simpler – and certainly less time consuming – than trying to explain it to each individual family member by phone.

Despite his unconditional love for his daughter, Rick was reminded of the orphans still needing help. Each time he looked at Nadia, he was filled with a joy that was tempered by his empathy for the other children. Just a few months after returning home with Nadia, Rick realized it was time to go back to Russia.

Although he had known he would return to Russia, Rick had not made any plans for the trip. In the early fall of 2003, Rick was at Vince's fortieth birthday party when, out of nowhere, this sudden sense of urgency overwhelmed him. He searched the room for his wife.

"Steph, I've got to leave for Russia as soon as possible," he said. She didn't blink or even register surprise. She just nodded as if he had told her he was running to the corner market for a loaf of bread.

Both Joe Lyons and Jimmy Huckaby were at the party, and Rick shared with both men his sudden urgency to return to Russia. He was touched by their response; both immediately asked to join him. Joe was eager to experience what had so profoundly touched Rick's life, and Jimmy wanted to film the experience. Rick was not sure, exactly, where this all was leading them, but he knew that there was more to the story than the documentary on Nadia.

They spent the next few weeks securing visas and passports for Jimmy and Joe, and Rick and Stephanie withdrew every penny they could from the bank. He knew the needs were great, but wasn't sure exactly what they would be. Because of this uncertainty, Rick told Jimmy and Joe, they would pray each day for God to lead them to where they needed to be and trust that they would be able to help.

The only game plan they had was to visit each orphanage, identify what that orphanage's greatest need was, and then see what they could do to address that need.

For Rick, the return was a sentimental one. Each leg of the journey now seemed so familiar, and he couldn't help but think about his first two visits here. His feelings were so different each time he had arrived in Moscow, and now he returned with a mission that differed in so many ways from his previous ones.

The three men arrived in Moscow on Friday, November 13, and they began their work by visiting the orphanages near Moscow. In Tula, south of Moscow, they visited a combination orphanage and school for children up to the age of young adulthood. Despite the clean conditions around him, the orphans' empty eyes haunted Rick. They seemed to cry out to him, begging for love and a better chance at life. From Tula, they journeyed to Novromoskov, an orphanage for children between the ages of three and seven years old.

Rick was not prepared for the sight he was about to experience; at first, he thought the building was abandoned, and he was stunned to discover it was a home for children. Inside, the kind but weary orphanage director explained that authorities had condemned the building, but they had nowhere else to go. Rick's eyes filled with tears as he looked at the sadness in their faces, and saw the leaking ceilings and exposed electrical wires. He couldn't imagine anyone living in such conditions – especially an innocent child!

Rick was silent as they made their way back to Moscow that night. The enormity of the task before him seemed overwhelming, and he knew that there were hundreds of more orphanages, thousands of more children who needed their help.

He walked the streets of Moscow alone that night, trying to clear his head and calling out for God to guide them. It was a gargantuan and ambitious task, but it was one he truly felt that God had placed in his heart. Rick knew he had to find a way to reach these children, not just one time, but to effectively change their world.

On Sunday night the three men began the twelve-hour journey by train to Pskov. As the train gently rocked its way through the Russian countryside, Rick revisited his emotions from the previous trips. He watched again as the sun came up and the farmers tended to their livestock. Those simple acts had already become familiar touchstones to him, providing a sort of comfort as if they, personally, were welcoming him back.

Ludmilla met them at the train station, and she was overjoyed to see Rick once more. They had stayed in constant contact since Rick's return home with Nadia. Ludmilla was sharing Nadia's story with everyone who would listen. When Jimmy completed his documentary, Rick had sent Ludmilla a DVD, which she showed to friends and translated into Russian for them. She found hope in Nadia's story, knowing that if one little girl could be saved, so can many others.

After a quick stop at the hotel, Ludmilla took them to the Kremlin to see the Minister of Education. She remembered Rick from his first visit, and she was touched to see that he had returned even after adopting the child he sought. This time, the Director of Education also joined them, and Rick shared the story of Nadia. He explained why he had felt compelled to return, and the two women told him just how important his mission was. Despite their gratitude for his help, they also explained that the one thing these children need most is the love of a family.

Rick's heart ached as the words resonated through him. He had been so blessed throughout his life, had always known the loving support of a family. It seemed so unfair that a child would have to grow up with anything less than that.

Ludmilla took the men to the Children's Hospital in Pskov, and Rick learned that every child who is orphaned or abandoned must first visit this hospital for evaluation and medical treatment. Through Ludmilla, he asked what their needs were. Rick's mind reeled at the list of items so often taken for granted. Thermometers, antibiotics, vitamins and even paper and pens were scarce. Over the next few days, Ludmilla took Rick, Joe and Jimmy all over the town in search of supplies and they bought a cache of medicines, books, paper, pens and even toys and games for the children.

They visited countless orphanages during their visit, and with each one it felt as if Rick's heart broke a little bit more. He was crushed by the lack of simple necessities that the children and their caregivers viewed as luxuries; fruit and juice were as rare a commodity as blankets and medicine. Once the lists were made, the small troupe would leave to find the supplies, returning to a hero's welcome from the children and looks of tearful disbelief from the workers.

It was Rick's return to the Pechory Children's Home that roused the deepest emotions within him. Making the now-familiar one-hour drive to the orphanage gave Rick plenty of time for reflection, and he marveled at how much his life had changed in such a short time. He could still feel the anticipation he had felt the first time he traveled across those beaten roads, and he could still feel the agony of being forced to leave Nadia behind. As they drove past the monastery, Rick caught his breath, knowing he was just a scant half-mile away from his daughter's former home.

As the car stopped in front of the orphanage, Rick's legs felt as weak as they had the first time he and Stephanie had visited Nadia. It was incomprehensible that Nadia had ever lived anywhere but in his own home. Rick felt awed and overpowered by all the events that had brought him to this point in his life.

Rick composed himself and followed Ludmilla up the stairs, flanked by Joe and Jimmy. As they entered the orphanage, the director saw Rick and began to cry.

"What? What is it?" he asked Ludmilla, who then spoke to the woman in Russian. The orphanage director tearfully answered her, and Ludmilla turned to Rick to explain.

"You came back," she said. "No one has ever come back before."

The simple words were overpowering to Rick. If he had ever doubted his need to wholeheartedly follow this mission, those words convinced him. He knew that this was just the beginning of his life's work, knew that everything he had done up until this point was merely a necessary part of a much bigger puzzle.

As with the other orphanages, the needs were staggering. The baby home where Nadia once had lived had no phone system to communicate with the outside world. Earlier that year, Rick had already been working to solve that problem. By the time he left Russia, the orphanage had its phone system as well as vacuum cleaners, baby walkers for the many disabled children living there, electric kettles to boil water and baby mobiles.

From one orphanage to the next, the lists continued and the purchases followed. Rick saw young children doing hard work. At one orphanage, he learned, children go to work at the age of three, beginning with such "simple" tasks as hauling debris and clearing the grounds. The men saw decrepit buildings trying to house small children, but the leaking roofs and collapsing floors were no match for Russia's harsh weather conditions.

What shocked Rick most about his visit was not the conditions the children lived in, but rather the hesitancy with which they were initially greeted. Each time they offered help, they were asked what they wanted in return. It saddened Rick to think that the only aid these people had been offered had come with strings attached, and it reinforced his determination to provide help without any conditions.

"We have to go forth, in the name of Christ, with no agenda, prerequisites or conditions," he told Jimmy and Joe. "We're here to touch the lives of children and to live by example. I don't think Jesus Christ would walk into an orphanage and say, 'If you accept me, then I'll help you.'"

He was outraged to hear that so many times, the aid offered had been contingent on a group being able to distribute literature or preach a message.

Rick knew that he had to base his work in Russia on living by example, not giving with an ulterior motive or agenda.

"We will never do that," he vowed to Joe and Jimmy. "I don't even want a thank-you. I just want to help those children."

After spending eleven days in Russia, Rick, Joe and Jimmy returned to Florida. All three of the men had been profoundly changed by their visit. Rick, in particular, rededicated his efforts to helping the one million orphans who were no longer just numbers to him. Determined to return again soon, Rick could not shake the faces of the children he had held. Where many people who had followed his story saw Nadia's arrival home as the end of a miracle, Rick now knew with complete certainty that she was only the beginning of a much larger one.

Nadia

Momma, Nadia and Pappa

Nadia and Rick at the Piano

Epilogue

The Project Anna Foundation continues working to create awareness of the problems facing Russian orphans and to provide assistance for those needs.

On April 29, 2004, Jimmy Huckaby's documentary, "Nadia's Story," won second place in the TV Documentary Short Film category at The International Family Film Festival Awards in Santa Clara, California.

Leaving on May 23, 2004 – one year to the day after Rick and Stephanie arrived in Russia to adopt Nadia – Rick and his son, Tony, journeyed to Russia. There, they continued the improvements The Project Anna Foundation had started in November 2003, providing money and supplies to numerous Russian orphanages.

Nadia continues to thrive in her new home, where she enjoys taking dance classes in addition to her other activities.

Rick remains dedicated to providing continued improvement for all of the children living in Russian orphanages, baby homes and hospitals. The goal of The Project Anna Foundation is to bring hope into the life of each child and to provide whatever is needed in terms of food, clothing, medical supplies and education.

Rick continues dreaming of the day when every orphanage in Russia will be empty.

For more information, please visit www.projectanna.org.